HANDICRAFTS IN ASSAM

HANDICRAFTS IN ASSAM

Krishna Jyoti Handique

KALPAZ

Handicrafts in Assam

Rs. 690

ISBN: 978-81-7835-819-2

Published in 2010 in India by
Kalpaz Publications
C-30, Satyawati Nagar,
Delhi-110052
E-mail: kalpaz@hotmail.com
Phone : 9212729499

Laser Type Setting by: Rudra Computer Graphics, Delhi
Printed at : Gian Ridhi Offset Printers, Delhi

Contents

Foreword

Traditionally rural artisans inherit craftsman skill but their is lack of professionalism among the artisans. Agriculture practice being seasonal, large number of the farm families find themselves out of employment during the lean agricultural seasons and they absorb themselves in different activities of handicrafts. The products of handicrafts are either used by the farm families or sold in the market. The important feature of the handicrafts in Assam is that these works not only provide income and partial employment opportunities to large number of rural families and full employment to many rural artisans but also exhibit an essential key to the understanding of cultural, social and religious heritage in the state. The professionalism still to emerge in this sector of the state in spite of the fact that cane and bamboo are easily available as raw materials for the crafts.

Dr. Handique's work in this area is a right approach in order to identity the problems and prospects of cane and bamboo crafts as profession.

The study will benefit the policy makers, researchers and NGOs who have addressed themselves in the study of the contribution of handicrafts sector of the national economy.

K.C. Borah
A Professor of Economics
Dibrugarh University, Dibrugarh
E-mail:-kcbecodu@rediffmail.com

Preface

The handicrafts have been playing an significant role in the economic development of Assam. Assam is very suitably endowed with resources for handicrafts in terms of men, materials and markets. The making of handicrafts products is relevant from the point of view of economic, environment and culture in Assam. There is an ample scope for the development of handicrafts on the basis of renewable resources in the state. The development of handicrafts will not only mobilize local resources but will also create employment and income opportunities for lakhs of people in the state. Although there is a potential for the development of handicrafts industry in Assam, some important constraint is always going against its expansion and growth. It therefore becomes imperative to identify steps to be taken to ensure the survival and growth of the handicrafts industry in liberalized economy. Keeping the above consideration in mind this study has been untaken to highlight the present status of handicrafts with particular reference to cane and bamboo works and seek to identify the promotional measures for the development of handicrafts industry, particularly cane and bamboo crafts in Assam.

This work is based on my Ph.D. thesis entitled "Handicrafts in Assam with Particular Reference to Cane and Bamboo Works" which has been awarded the Doctor of Philosophy Degree in Economics from Dibrugarh University, Dibrugarh. The study would not have been possible for me without the co-operation and help of a number of persons, organizations and institutions. I have no words to expresses my deep sense of gratitude and indebtedness to the supervisor of this study, Professor Kumud Chandra Borah, Department of Economics, Dibrugarh University, Dibrugarh under whose able guidance I completed my research work. I express my indebtedness to my father Mr. Jadav Handique and mother Mrs. Rupahi Handique who had been a constant source of inspiration from the beginning till the completion of my study. I also extend my thanks to my brothers Mr. Dhurba Jyoti Handique and Mr. Naba Jyoti Handique for their help and encouragement. I awe nonrefundable debt to my wife Mrs. Poli Handique, Lecturer in the Department of Education, Gargaon College, Simaluguri for untiring support and patience throughout my research work. I am also grateful to Mr. Lohit Chandra Konwar, Supervising Assistant, Gargaon College, Simaluguri for his immense help to bring out this work in the present from.

I wish to express my indebtedness to state and central government officials of different connected to like Development Commissioner (Handicrafts), Ministry of Textile, Government of India and Department of Industries and Commerce, Government of Assam for their valuable co-operation during the period of the study.

Finally, I would crave the indulgence of the reader for the unintentional errors that might have crept in spite of my sincere care.

Krishna Jyoti Handique
July, 2009

List of Tables

The first digit of the Table Number stands for the Chapter to which the particular Table belongs, while the second and third digit indicates the serial numbers of that Table in that Chapter

1

Introduction

The handicrafts have a deep significance to our society in day-to-day life of the people. It is seen that handicrafts stand as an example of human creativity expressed over generating of human society. It may be mentioned that from the beginning of the known human history, the handicrafts form a valuable social, cultural and economic trait of a community. The socio-economic pattern of a society is very often reflected in the quality, creativity and craftsmanship of handicrafts. The handicrafts not only constitute the economic life but also the cultural unity of the people. It is a fact that the handicrafts items have far greater significance than is indicated by the value of their production as they embody cultural, social, religious and artistic traditions in the society.

The term handicrafts stand for those items of a specific society, which are generally produced manually with their traditional indigenous technical knowledge. Handicrafts tell us about the nature and needs of life of the people which are the indigenous creation and expression of the rural folk. In certain parts of the world, handicrafts have been the skilled work, to create items of utility. However, the activities of handicraft can be termed as trade or occupation that requires to develop skill in the use of mind and hand. In most of the developing countries, handicrafts have continued in their traditional forms.

Handicrafts have been defined in different ways. In the report of the Task Force on handicrafts, for eight five year plan, it has been rightly observed that it is difficult to give a cut-and-dried definition on handicrafts.[1] Various Organizations and writers have given different definitions of handicrafts in a different manner from time to time. According to Encyclopedia Britannica, "handicrafts are manual skills for making usable products graced with international visual appeal."[2] In the New Book of Knowledge, handicrafts have been defined as "objects made by hand, usually one at a time, are handicrafts."[3] The office of the Development Commissioner (Handicrafts), Ministry of Textiles, Govt. of India, New Delhi, has given a workable definition on handicrafts as "items made by hand, often with the use of simple tools, and generally artistic and/or traditional in nature. They include objects of utility and objects of decoration"[4]. In the words of M.P. Ranjan, "the term handicrafts and Crafts are used in a very specific sense, to mean those activities that deal with the conversion of materials into products, using primarily hands skills with simple tools and employing the local tradition wisdom of craft Processed"[5]. On the other hand, John Mao mentioned that "the term craft has been derived from the Anglo-Saxon craft which means skill, strength or cunning in contrast to art which implies an intention of producing beauty or pleasure"[6]. From the above definitions, it can be mentioned here that the range of studying handicrafts are very wide because it includes all the activities or objects that produce, by using hand skills with simple tools and mind. In fact, handicrafts should cover products made primarily by hands skills with simple tools; use of mind and employing indigenous knowledge. Handicrafts were originally made for home consumption, but occasionally, some surplus products were exchanged for goods. With the changes of economic system handicraft products were sold into the market economy.

Depending on their various specialization, the maker of crafts known as artisan, craftsmen, craftsperson, designer crafts parson, artist craftsperson etc. Kanwarjit Nagi has used the word craftsperson to imply a skilled worker in crafts[7]. Dictionary of Economics has defined craftsman as "a skilled worker in a particular occupation, trade or crafts, who is able to apply a range of skills to basically non-repetitive work with a minimum of direction and supervision."[8]. It may be mentioned that a person who has engaged himself for production of handicrafts items with the help of his hand, eye, brain and tools for both home consumption and business purposes is generally known as handicrafts artisan or craftsman. This definition is also applied to the craftsman in Assam. In Assam, the crafts objects are generally created by the tribal craftsmen, mainly or partly, according to their traditional pattern.

The handicrafts not only provide income and employment opportunities to lakhs of people but also an essential key to the understanding of the cultural, social and religious heritage in the state of Assam. The skilled hand of a craftsman is most important and most the invisible resource of a society. According to Encyclopedia Britannica, handicrafts includes needle work, lace, weaving, printed textile, pottery, ornamental, metalwork, jewelry, leatherwork, wood working, embroidered goods, cane, bamboo, bell-metal, ivory, tannery works etc[9]. A Catalogue on Handicrafts of India includes handloom woven fabrics and hand printed artistic cotton and silk textiles, bamboo and cane works, wood carving, ivory and horn works, handloom, leather works, pottery, jewellery and metal wares and a host of such other artistic products of cottage artisans as handicrafts.[10] In the context of industry and crafts, it can be mentioned that industry has its origin in crafts. In the Pre Industrial Age, agriculture and handicrafts were interdependent and combined and the degree of the development of crafts in a country was dependent on agricultural development. T. M. Abraham observed that "craft is the historical parent of modern industry and the craftsman was the immediate predecessor to the modern industrial technologist."[11] It is a fact that the primary aim of a craftsman is perfection of beauty in the product of his hand and mind. At the same time, a craftsman is like a poet or a painter in a society. From the social points of view, handicrafts are essential for the satisfaction of human wants. Handicrafts satisfy not only the economic wants alone but also the aesthetic cravings of human hearth throughout the world.

Among the various crafts, cane and bamboo works are the most important crafts in India. At the same time, Assam is very suitably endowed with resources for cane and bamboo works in terms of men, material and markets. Assam has been blessed with very rich, important tropical resources including cane and bamboo. It may be noted that cane and bamboo are now considered as the most important natural and renewable vegetable resources in the world. Cane and bamboo works are also recognized for a sustainable development in the economy of Assam. From the very ancient times, cane and bamboo works have been recognized as the most important works because of its role in ecological, social, cultural and economic up-liftmen of people of Assam. Among the famous traditional crafts, the making of cane and bamboo items is perhaps the most universally practiced by all sections of the people throughout the state of Assam[12]. The cane and bamboo crafts bear the witness of many cultures, traditions, races and civilization and these have been persevered by the long experience of cane and bamboo skilled artisan of Assam. The cane and bamboo product may be termed as pure handicraft products and these products have very wide range of uses and such commodities are found in every household in the state. The wide range of utility of cane and bamboo products has the sanction of tradition and culture in the state.

Assam is one of the most important states of India known for its rich and diverse cane and bamboo products. The state has been blessed with very rich and important tropical resource including cane and bamboo from the very ancient time. It is generally seen that cane and bamboo products are part and parcel of the life of the people of Assam. The cane and bamboo items are used extensively in the day-to-day life of people throughout the state which provides more employment opportunities and better income distribution to the people.. This craft is mainly a household cottage industry and it provides a subsidiary occupation of the rural people. On the other hand, this craft provides full-time occupation to those highly skilled artisans who produce cane and bamboo products on commercial basis in both rural and urban areas in Assam. The potentiality of making cane and bamboo articles on commercial scale is quite considerable for the good demand in the state.

Assam has a rich diversity in cane and bamboo resources. It may be mentioned here that there are over 1200 species of bamboo found in the world. The largest bamboo resources covering 500 species of bamboo are found in China. Whereas in India, 120 species of bamboo are reported.[13] On the other hand, about 600 species of cane are found in the world. Indonesia is one of the largest supplier of raw cane comprising about 300 species. It is known that 51 species of cane are distributed in different part of India[14]. The North Eastern Region occupies more than 50 percent of the total bamboo area with 81 species of bamboo. It is known that more then 24 species of cane are found in different areas of the North Eastern Region. On the other hand, about 18 species of cane (Appendix I) and about 29 species of bamboo (Appendix II) are available in the state of Assam[15]. It is generally seen that despite the diverse species of cane and bamboo, only a handful and suitable species are used by the artisans in Assam. Some cane and bamboo species are cultivated in homesteads and some species are grown naturally in the forest of Assam. Our cane and bamboo artisans collect their valuable raw materials for handicraft industries, mostly from homesteads, local market and nearby natural forests of the sate. The cane and bamboo industry is generally a low capital but labour intensive and hence acts as a good employment generation and better income distribution to the people. These household industries provide diverse employment opportunities and value-added products in every rural household.

It is a fact that the cottage industry can play a major role to reduce unemployment, poverty and income inequalities problems in the third world countries, like India. The manufacturing activities of cane and bamboo crafts in most of the rural areas of Assam are carried out by both male and female members of the family, but the male members pre-dominate the activities of cane and bamboo works. The manufacturing of most of the products is meant for domestic use and only a small part of the products is sold in the market. There are large number of units in the urban and semi-urban areas engaged in the manufacture of various cane and bamboo products with distinctive features and exquisite designs. The making of cane and bamboo products requires a high degree of skill and knowledge. In these cane and bamboo units, the professional artisans are associated who follow this trade as a whole time occupation sell their products in the different markets. It may be recalled that the cane and bamboo are used for the construction of houses, bridges, various kind of household utility items, fishing instruments, musical implements, weaving implements, decorative items, ploughing instruments, hunting implements etc. for the daily usage of the Assamese People. The cane and bamboo articles like *Bahi, Bichani, Bor-chunga, Chepa, Chalani, Charakee, Cheri, Dola, Doon, Dhara, Dhanu, Duli, Dingaru, Gagona, Garaka, Hukuma, Hali, Japi, Jakoi, Jluki, Japa, Kula, Khorahi, Karia, Lati, Khuka, Khaloi, Latai, Murha, Muhura, Pawra, Pachi, Pola, Ranch, Tuna, Thoura, Toka, Ugha,* Flower Vase, Fruit Tray, Tea Tray, Candle Stand, Magazine Rack, Flower Basket, Tea Stainer, Beer Mug, Jewellery Box, Hanger, Egg Shape Basket, Umbrella Stand, Baby Jhula, Baby Cot, Garden Chair, Dining Chair, Ladies hand mirrors, etc., are used extensively for day to day life of the people of Assam.

The Assamese craftsmen like other part of the world have been practicing cane and bamboo culture since time immemorial by using various techniques. To know about the material culture of the Assamese people, it is essential to study the cane and bamboo crafts evolution which have cut a deep impression in the life of the people in Assam. Of the exquisite designs of cane and bamboo items, some are made for general use and some are made for sale in the market. However, with the changing socio-economic scenario artisans have begun to sell in the markets those items that are required in everyday life of the people. It can be noted here that in most of the cane and bamboo growing developing countries, cane and bamboo crafts have continued as a folk craft. A.G. Rao observed that folk crafts which catered to the needs of the rural population, have remained simple and the creativity of folk craft excelled in harmonious social settings[16]. The creativity of the artisans have reflected in the high level of product aesthetics. It is now known that cane and bamboo craft is an integral part of the culture, traditions and the religious ceremonies in most of the South Asian countries. It also provides one of the items of food, raw materials, shelter and even medicine for a good part of the population in the world. In Japan, bamboo is treated as a precious material akin to gold and almost cares and attention has been given to the artisan's work, which is reflected in the exquisite quality and craftsmanship of the Japanese bamboo items. Cane is also considered one of the most important minor forest products in India. It is however estimated that there has been increasing growth of cane-trade in Indonesia, Philippines, Malaysia and Thailand, over the past decade, but there was an declining trend in India.

The cane and bamboo craft has been an inseparable and indispensable part of the economy of Assam as well as NER. The making of cane and bamboo handicrafts becomes crucially relevant from the angle of economic, environment, employment, equality and culture in Assam. The cane and bamboo craft constitutes an important sector in the rural areas for the earning of income of the rural folk. With the changing Socio-economic scenario, the craft is shifting from rural to urban areas in the state. However, the cane and bamboo craft is functioning in an unorganized way. The cane and bamboo products are in great demand outside the state. But the supply can not be increased due to old aged method of production. It has been widely believed that handicrafts industry has a special place in the economic development of Assam. Of course, the role perceived for crafts including cane and bamboo crafts and the nature of crafts has been changing over time, but the importance attached to it in the developmental process remains unsatisfactory in Assam. At the same time, it is also seen that the cane and bamboo products are representative of a major fraction of the rich diversity of handicrafts of Assam which constitute an indigenous cottage industry in the state of Assam.

Importance of the Study:

In a backward state like Assam, handicrafts have a big role to play for economic development. There is ample scope for the development of handicrafts on the basis of factor endowments available in the state. The rural agricultural families of the state earn supplementary income from different types of handicrafts. Among the various crafts, cane and bamboo works are the most important crafts in Assam. The cane and bamboo works not only provide employment and income opportunities but also form a prominent element in cultural and social unity of the Assamese people. The cane and bamboo artisans have been important element in the development process of the state. From the very ancient times, handicrafts had been recognized as the most important economic activity in the state. Therefore, a comprehensive study on handicrafts assumes great relevance and significance.

The importance of cane and bamboo works as remunerative economic activity is yet to be realized in Assam. The cane and bamboo works are amenable to labour intensive and value added processing systems. As cane and bamboo products enter divers markets, the value of these resources tends to grow in the state. Additional benefits may be derived from cane and bamboo works, systematized resource use, management, marketing and processing in the state. In Assam, handicrafts study have been shown by some writers, departments, organizations etc,. But very few systematic studies on the potentiality of cane and bamboo works have been made in Assam. Only recently some scholars and the very few organizations have shown their interest in assessing the present status and potentiality of cane and bamboo works in the state. The scope of our study covers problems and prospects of handicrafts in Assam, particularly cane and bamboo works. It is hope that such research study will also enrich knowledge, especially in the field of handicrafts in the state. We also hoped that such knowledge will lead to overcome the different socio-economic barriers in the handicrafts sector in Assam.

Objectives of the Study:

In spite of abundance of raw materials for cane and bamboo crafts in the state, crafts based on cane and bamboo works are not developed, as expected. The professionalisation in the handicrafts industry has yet not started in the state. Instead, much of the traditional items made from cane and bamboo are fast disappearing from the state. The present study seeks to modest attempt to examine the following objectives.

1. To study the historical development and present status of handicrafts in the state.

2. To find out the socio-economic conditions of the cane and bamboo entrepreneurs.

3. To find out economics of cane and bamboo units.

4. To examine the problems and prospects of cane and bamboo works in the state.

5. To assess the overall status of cane and bamboo works in Assam in order to formulate strategies for its growth in competitive market.

Hypotheses:

To fulfill these objectives, the following hypotheses will be tested.

1. Cane and bamboo works are not remunerative to the entrepreneurs in Assam.

2. There is no proper infrastructural facilities for development of cane and bamboo works in Assam.

Methodology:

In order to achieve the objectives of the present study, seven districts were selected for field investigation from the Brahmaputra valley in Assam. These seven districts were purposively selected for field investigation as cane and bamboo works are mostly concentrated in these districts. These seven districts are Sivasagar, Tinsukia, Nagaon, Nalbari, Sonitpur, Kamrup and Goalpara district of the state. These districts are located at the Brahmaputra valley of Assam. The list of registered cane and bamboo units in the rural and urban areas of the seven districts was prepared. From the list only a few successful units were purposively selected. For non registered units the efficiently functioning units as reported by the District Industrial Centre and Commerce (DICC) were purposively selected. All total 131 cane and bamboo units were randomly selected from both rural and urban areas for collection of primary data from the seven districts for the purpose of this study. Out of the total 131 sample units, 86 (65.65%) were rural and the rest of 45(34.35%) were in the urban area. This present study is an empirical research based on the survey method. The primary data relating to cane and bamboo units has been collected through personal interview method. For the purpose of collection of primary data, a survey schedule (Appendix III) has been used. District wise sample cane and bamboo units are presented in Table 1.1.

The randomly selected total 131 cane and bamboo units for primary data collection were both registered and non-registered units. Out of the total 35 registered units, 18(51.43 %) were rural and 17(48.57 %) were urban areas of the surveyed districts.

The primary information collected through canvassing the survey schedule among the sample cane and bamboo units were aggregated and then the collected data were properly processed and tabulated by using standard statistical tools for the purpose of analysis in the

Table: 1.1

District wise of Sample Cane and Bamboo Units, 2002-03

District	*No. of Rural Units*			*No. of Urban Units*			*No. of Total Units*
	Registered Units	*Non Registered Units*	*No. of Total Rural Units*	*Registered Units*	*Non Registered Units*	*No. of Total Urban Units*	
Sivasagar	3	14	17	4	5	9	26
Tinsukia	2	11	13	2	2	4	17
Nagaon	2	8	10	3	4	7	17
Nalbari	4	9	13	2	2	4	17
Sonitpur	3	12	15	2	3	5	20
Kamrup	2	9	11	3	3	6	17
Goalpara	2	5	7	1	9	10	17
Total	18	68	86 **(65.65)**	17	28	45 **(34.35)**	131

present study. To supplement the primary data the secondary data for the present study has been collected from both Government and Non-Government sources. A number of discussions have been held with reliable and learned persons such as government officials, industrialists, artisans, traders, middleman and workers employed in the cane and bamboo units in the state in order to know the inside of the present status of cane and bamboo units in the state.

Statistical Tools Used:

The concept of profit/volume ratio (P/V ratio) is applied to calculate the break-even point (BEP) (in terms of sale) from cane and bamboo works of the sample units. The equation of the P/V ratio is expressed as under.

$$\text{P/V ratio} = \frac{S - V}{S}$$

This P/V ratio is shown in the form of percentage by multiplying 100. Thus

$$\text{P/V ratio} = \frac{S - V}{S} \times 100$$

The equation of BPE (in terms of sale) is fitted as under

$$\text{BEP} = \frac{FC}{\text{P/V ratio}}$$

Where, S means sales, V means variable cost and FC means fixed cost

Reference Period:

A fixed one year reference period from July 2002 to June 2003 was used for all surveyed units. Thus, the reference period of these data is 2002-03.

Limitations of the Study:

It is true that in spite of our sincere effort, the study is subject to certain limitations. The present study is confined to seven districts having predominance of cane and bamboo crafts for the primary data collection. The handicrafts sector is mostly in the unorganized sector of the state. It is a well known fact that the handicrafts sector is run by mostly uneducated and less educated persons in general. Usually, the cane and bamboo artisans do not care to maintain records of production, consumption, investment and marketing etc. However, the collected data have been verified from various reliable sources in this study. Care was taken for the collection and verification of necessary data. In spite of the mentioned shortcomings the present study is expected to fill an important gap of fact finding and throw new light regarding the problems and prospects in the handicrafts sector in the state.

Layout of the Study:

The study report has been organized into seven chapters.

The first chapter deals primarily with the introduction and design of the study. This chapter covers introduction, importance of the study, objectives of the study, hypotheses, methodology, reference period, limitation of the study and layout of the study.

The second chapter has objectively examined the historical development of handicrafts in Assam. This chapter also deals with the present status of cane and bamboo works in the state.

The third chapter deals with review of literature on handicrafts in general and cane and bamboo works in particular. The important research study, survey and committee reports, relevant to our study have been reviewed in this chapter.

Chapter four has been devoted to analysis in socio-economic conditions of the sample entrepreneurs of the cane and bamboo units along with the socio-economic profile of the surveyed districts.

The fifth chapter covers the assessments of the economics of cane and bamboo units.

The sixth chapter deals with the identification of the various problems of the cane and bamboo works and the discussion of prospects of developing cane and bamboo works in the state.

The last chapter provides the main findings, suggestions for development of cane and bamboo works in the state and conclusions of the present study.

References

1. Saraf D.N., *Craft Development, 1941-1991,* Sampark, New Delhi, 1991, p. 46.

2. *Encyclopedia Britannica*, INC, Publisher Chicago, 1966, Vol. II, p. 58.

3. *The New Book of knowledge*, Grolier Incorporated, Connecticut, USA, 1994, Vol. VI, pp. 78-79.

4. Lierl, Maureen and Ray, Tirthankar., "Handmade in India: Preliminary Analysis of crafts producers and crafts Production", *Economic and Political Weekly,* Mumbai, 2003, Vol. XXXVIII, p. 5367.

5. Ranjan, M.P., *"Green Design and Bamboo Handicrafts: a scenario for Research and Action in the Asian Region"*, in Rad, Ramanuja IV and Sastry, Cherla. B (ed.), *"Bamboo, People and the Environment,"* Proceeding of the 5th international Bamboo congress Ubud , Bali, Indonesia, 19-22 June 1995, Vol. 3, Engineering and Utilization, International Development Research Centre, Canada, 1996, p. 313.

6. Mao, John, *"Traditional craft and Technology in Manipur,"* in Singh Jai Prakash (ed.), *"Archaeology of North-Eastern Region,"* Vikas Publishing House Pvt. Ltd. New Delhi, 1991, p. 319.

7. Nagi, Kanwarjit., The status of Bamboo and Bamboo craft in Karjat, India, and Strategies for Development, INBAR working paper No. 19, International Network for Bamboo and Ralttan, New Delhi, 1998, p. I.

8. Madian, M.C. (ed.), *Dictionary of Economics*, Himalaya Publishing house, Delhi, 1997, p. 65.

9. *Encyclopedia Britannica*, op. cit., p. 58.

10. Baishya, Prabin., *Small and Cottage Industries*, A study in Assam, Manas Publications, Delhi, 1989, p. 168.

11. Abraham, T.M., *Handicrafts in India*, Graphics Columbia, New Delhi, 1964, p. 32.

12. *Assam State Gazetteer*, Vol. I, Govt. of Assam, Guwahati, 1999, p. 440.

13. Haridasan, K., "Bamboo Based Socio Economic Revolution in Rural South Eastern China-Relevance to North East

India," *Arunachal Forest News*, Vol. 18, Itanagar, 2000, p. 41.

14. Lakshurana, A.C., *Rattans of South Indian*, Evergreen publishers, Bangalore, 1993, p. 1.

15. *Study of Cane and Bamboo Reserve in North East India*, Technical Report, North Eastern Handicrafts and Handloom Development Corporation, Shillong, 2001, p. 12.

16. Rao, A.G., "*Design Inputs into Craft Areas: Implications for Rural Development and Employment Generation*," In Rao, Ramanuja. IV and Sastry, Cherla. B (ed.), "*Bamboo, People and the Environment*," Proceeding of the Vth International Bamboo Congress, Ubud, Bali, Indonesia, 19-22 June 1995, Vol. 3, Engineering and Utilization, International Development Research Centre, Canada, 1996, p. 287.

2

Handicrafts in Assam: Past and Present

2.1. Development of Handicrafts in India:

The development of handicrafts in India is as old as the country itself. The "traditions of many crafts in our country can trace their origins back almost to about 5000 year ago, to the ancient Indus valley and Mohenjo-Daro civilizations, and they have been created and developed through the ages against a background that is richly woven with the synthesis of many cultures, myths and imagery of sign and symbol."[1] In the ancient times, handicrafts had been recognized as the most important economic activity in our country. The village artisan became an integral part within the social, economic and religious fabric of the way of life in ancient India. In the Gupta Period, each village had its own blacksmith, potter, carpenter, skinner of dead cattle, tanner, barber and so on.[2]

Like the classical era of the Guptas, the Maghuls encouraged and promoted handicrafts in India. The craftsmen showed excellent skill in the making of handicrafts products in the Moghul period. It is known that "Akbar brought skilled craftsman from other countries and picked Hindu experts from India"[3] However, Indian handicrafts had received less attention from the British rulers. The establishment of British rules in India was the cause of disruption of the age-old indigenous manufacturing industry, town handicrafts and village artisan industries.[4] The growth of factory system of mass production was the major cause for the progressive decline of the century old Indian handicrafts. The establishment of new industries by the British government destroyed the traditional opportunities for handicrafts. The import of foreign made - products affected the artisans and they had lost their simple but happy life after the factory of production in India.

When colonialism started to spread, the artisans were pushed back into agriculture. It extremely over-crowded the agriculture sector. In ancient India, craftsmens' lives were very happy, because crafts were highly encouraged and supported by the royalty. But the craftsmen had lost their comfortable life and earnings during the last decades of the nineteenth century in India

After 1857, the Swadeshi movement was gradually started and it encouraged and advocated the use of Indian made handicrafts products and boycott of foreign goods in India. The more significance was that the revival of cultural heritage of crafts was made a part of the national freedom movement by M.K. Gandhi. In the address made by Kamaladevi Chattopadhyay at the First World Congress of Craftsmen, New York, June 1964, She pointed out that "the national regeneration of the people, as Gandhiji Visualised it, was to come through the re-creation of their ideals, aspirations and dreams shaped partly through living objects of craftsmanship, the creative impulse comes from the people and is infused into their undertakings"[5] After independence, the national government had taken positive effort for the development and improvement of handicrafts in our country.

2.2. Development of Handicrafts in Assam:

In ancient Assam, the handicrafts like working in metal, ivory, wood, leather, clay, cane, bamboo and the like and their reputation was almost equal to that of the craftsmen of other parts of contemporary India. Many kinds of master craftsmen emerged in different professional classes, like weavers, spinners, goldsmiths, potters and workers in ivory, wood, cane and bamboo. Old literates, epigraph, foreign accounts, manuscripts etc. proving that handicrafts had played an important role in the daily life of the Assamese people in ancient days. It is known that the famous Chinese traveler Hiuen Tsiang visited to the capital of Bhaskara Varman in about 643 A.D. in Kamrupa. Then Hiuen Tsiang had received handicrafts gifts from the famous king Bhaskara Varman of Kamrupa[6]. The Chinese traveler Hiuen Tsiong recorded descriptions of handicrafts in Assam which he received as gifts from the illustrious king Bhaskara Varman of Kamrupa. It can be noted that after the visit of Hiuen Tsiong, handicrafts of Assam won wide appreciation from other travelers in the state.

After the thirteenth century, handicrafts had reached a very high point of perfection under the Ahom kings in Assam. The different professional classes, like weavers, spinners, dyers, smith, workers in ivory, metal, wood, jewellery and pottery enjoyed state patronage and the villages were developed on the basis of these classes. Most of the artisans followed their hereditary pursuits and they had local and traditional technology. Crafts production was on local consumption level. The artisan made handicrafts products for mainly home consumption, but occasionally some surplus products were supplied to the king's household and some products were exchanged particularly for goods. In the medieval period, besides the professional craftsmen, some villagers started making a verity of bamboo baskets, fishing appliances and containers which were locally bartering for salt, oil, arecanuts, rice and such other necessaries of life.[7] There were no guilds of craftsman in Assam but the king made ***khel*** system, specifying a particular profession. In the early seventeenth century, the Ahom king Pratap Simha, artisans from Koch Behar were brought to teach new techniques and designs to the local artisans. In the medieval period, the *satra* institution had also played an important role for the development of various indigenous crafts in Assam. In the hills areas of Assam the tribal handicrafts were interwoven with the social life of the family.

Among the various crafts, cane and bamboo works gained its popularity during the medieval period of Assam. The Ahoms, Kacharis, Kochs, Bodos, Mikirs, Miris and other ethnic groups had their own traditions on cane and bamboo handicrafts. Cane and bamboo were mainly used for the construction of houses and various kind of fishing items, cultivation instruments, weaving instruments, construction bridges, weapons, musical instruments etc. These were used in the daily life of the Assamese people in the medieval period. Some varieties of cane and bamboo were cultivated and some were naturally grown. The different cane and bamboo species were used by the artisans for various purposes according to their suitability, quality, durability, girth and length. In fact, cane and bamboo resources played a dominant role in almost all aspects of the life of the people. The craftsmen could collect cane free of cost from the forest in the hill as well as plains of Assam..

The artistic items were made from cane and bamboo, which were used for domestic purpose. In those days, the most beautiful and artistic items of various types of ***japi*** were made with cane and bamboo. The general type of ***japi*** was the most indispensable item for the cultivator. The decorated and artistic ***japi*** like ***barjapi***, ***tapijapi*** and ***sarudaiyajapi*** were used by the nobles accordingly to their ranks in the Ahom period.[8] These ***japis*** were ornamented and embroidered with various designs indicative of the dignity and social status of those using them in the medieval period. The royal patronage of cane and bamboo works during the period of the Ahom Kings were evident from the rules executed by the officials. Momai Tamuli Barbarua, a prominent minister of king Pratap Sinha (1603-1614), made it compulsory on the part of every adult male for making of bamboo basket in the Ahom Period.

In the medieval period, the *satra* institution also contributed to the development of cane and bamboo crafts in Assam. Training in cane and bamboo works were also provided by the *satras*. The famous ***bichani*** made from cane in Auniati *satra* signified the skilled obtained by the craftsman in the *satra* institution. The artistic cane and bamboo works in the *satras* bore the witness of high order of craftsmanship in Assam. Generally, cane and bamboo items were made for home consumption, but with the change of economic situations occasionally some items were sold in the market.

Other crafts those of pottery, goldsmith, blacksmith, weaving, brass, metal, bell metal, sital pati, solapith, kuhila, koth, stone works, wood works, ivory works, leather works etc. in Assam were highly developed and played a significant role in the social, cultural and economic life of the people in the medieval period. Pottery was the hereditary practice by Kumar and Hira communities. The Kumars used the wheel for the making of pottery articles and the Hiras made these articles by hand without the wheel, in Assam. During the medieval period, varieties of valuable ornaments had been produced by the goldsmiths in Assam. Gold was found in the sand of some rivers. The gold washers from the sand of the rivers were known as Sonowals a schedule tribe community of Assam. The Ahom king Pratap Sinha brought goldsmiths from Koch Behar and his successor king Rudra Sinha brought goldsmiths from Banares to teach new technique and design to the Assamese goldsmiths[9]. Blacksmithy was a common craft and the people who practiced in this hereditary profession were known as kamars.

Assam had a high tradition and reputation in weaving craft in the medieval period. Every Assamese family practiced spinning yarn and weaving cloth. In the Koch Kingdom the professional silk spinners and weavers were known as Katanis.[10] In the Ahom period, the able minister Momai Tamuli Barbarua made it obligatory that "before sunset every woman must spin certain number of hands of yarn."[11] A community of Assam known as Mariya produced brass metal articles in the medieval period. Bell-metal manufacturing was also a hereditary profession and the bell-metal workers were known as Kahar. In this connection it may be mentioned here that the Ahome king Siba Sinha (1714-1744) in recognition of expertise of making bell-metal items presented Jiudhan Kahar of Sarthebari a 'tamrapatra' with the tittle 'Kahar Choudhury' and donated 40 bighas of revenue free land for his used[12].

Among the other handicrafts, mention may be made of ***sital-pati***, solapith and kuhila koth were the important handicrafts in some areas of medieval Assam. In the medieval period, people used ***sital-pati*** for sleeping and sitting. Mohapurush Madhavdev made the first kuhila koth in Assam.[13] Similarly, under the Ahom rule there was significance development of wood works carried on to a large extent with the patronage of the kings and the *satras*. There were many wood workers in the village that made various kinds of wood works for the use of daily life of the people. The wood and timber workers were called Khanikar and they produced articles like ***palang, salpira, barpira, para, dula, garu ason, jatar*** etc. During the fifteenth century wood works in Assam were significantly developed. Sankaradeva the famous vaisnavite leader of Assam engaged Karala Barhai to carve out a wooden Visnu image which was installed with a religious ceremony in the ***namghar***.[14] Assam was also famous for ivory works in the medieval period. Both the plains and hills people made different kinds of beautiful ivory items. The bordering tribal kings supplied abundant quantities of ivory to the Ahom Kings. It is recorded that the Ahom King Rudra Sinha sent mats and fans which were made of ivory to Mughal Emperor in Delhi as gift[15]. The *mukha* craft was famous in the medieval times. Mahapurush Sankardeva created the first mukha craft for vaisnavite movement in Assam .Besides, many people were engaged in leather works, silver works, copper works, dyeing, lime, brick making, working on rhinoceros and buffalo horns etc., which were widely appreciated in Assam. In order to bring about stability in handicrafts the Ahom Kings in many occasion, establishment various traditional handicrafts workers at different places in medieval period of Assam.

This account of various crafts practiced by the people revealed that crafts played a very prominent role for the self-sufficient economic system in medieval Assam. In the seventeenth century the French traveler J.P. Tavernier observed that "the kingdom of Assam is one of the best countries in Asia, for it products all that is necessary to the life of the man without there being need to go for anything to the neighboring states"[16]. This evidence also goes to show the importance the handicrafts had acquired in the changing of economic life of the people in medieval Assam. It is a fact that towards the closing decades of the Ahom kings due to the Mayamara rebellions and Burmese invasions the crafts traditions considerably weakened in Assam.

In 1826, the British took over Political Power in Assam. In the beginning of the British rules the handicrafts were in most cases combined with agriculture. Most of the artisans continued with their hereditary pursuits which was passed on by tradition from father to son. Gradually, the demand for the handicrafts products declined, as the new rich classes during the period of nineteenth century preferred handicrafts made in the foreign countries to the native products for social and political reasons. The traditional crafts started declining for the adoption of free trade in that period. The expansion of free trade resulted in increased demand of foreign made products in Assam. In the words of H. K. Borpujari, "brass-copper-iron wares, mats ivory works continued to be exported from Assam until 1835. In subsequent years, exports constituted mostly of the raw materials while the import of foreign goods was on the increase"[17]. The decline of the Ahom government saw the disappearance of patronage enjoyed by the artisans in Assam. In the British Period, the development of new industries, roads, railway, telegraphs etc., increased the competition between local products and foreign made products and hastened the process of the decline of handicrafts in Assam.

The neglect of the traditional crafts by the British government helped in developing and benefiting the modern industries. In the time of growth of modern industries, such a situation arose that local artisans were being steadily pushed out by imported items in the state. With the introduction of new tools and machines there had been a change in the traditional craftsmanship.

Under the new socio-economic system, the indigenous handicrafts were also continuously practiced as a household industries by some of the people in Assam. In that time, in the agrarian society of Assam it was seen that most of the cultivators were partly dependent for their living on the products of traditional handicrafts. But early 20th century, gradually, the numbers of persons employed in the handicrafts were decreased noteworthy as their products could not compete with the machine made products. The census of 1891 records show that there were only four ivory workers in Assam.[18] Similarly, the 1901 census revels that there were only four wood and ebony carvers in Assam. Traditionally many people were engaged gold and silver works. The 1901 census reveled that in the manufacture and sale of silver and gold ornaments the number of persons employed were 14956 in the state.[19] It is difficult to know the actual earnings of the local artisans since they also bartered their products in exchange of occasionally other products. Edward Gait mentioned that the Potters' monthly income did not exceed six rupees.[20] In the closing of the nineteenth century cane and bamboo were exported from Assam. Like other crafts, making of cane and bamboo items were subsidiary occupations to the cultivators. In the rural areas, every family made at least a part of its domestic requirement of cane and bamboo articles. Crafts like black smithy, carpentry, weaving, gold smithy, pottery, brass and bell metal etc. were mostly associated with the village economy.

In the whole British role traditional handicrafts had continuously received a negligent treatment from the British in Assam. There was colonial pattern of economic development at that time, which discouraged traditional handicrafts in the state. The indigenous artisans making articles faced stiff competition with imported high quality of machine made articles. Under such a situation many artisans closed down their handicrafts work-shops. For the declining of traditional handicrafts the artisans undertaking agriculture as their occupation in the state. owever, it was only after the first world war that the government realized the importance of traditional handicrafts in the economy of Assam.

After the first world war, a separate department of industries was established for giving adequate support for the promotion of traditional industries in the state. The establishment of separate government department for the development of traditional industries, however helped the expansion of handloom weaving and sericulture industries in Assam only. There was no such evidence of improvement the traditional industries including handicrafts in those days. It is known that following the decision of the Indian nationalists, Assamese nationalist leaders also called upon the people of boycotting the foreign made goods and the use of only swadeshi goods during the time of national movement. The national movement gave an opportunity to the artisans to work again and create artistic activity of crafts, many of which had been through the ages in the society. In 1918, eminent social worker Bhuban Chandra Gogoi established a technical school at Patsaku in Sivasagar district of his own initiative. Later, this school was transferred to Sivasagar town in 1923. Some handicrafts like blacksmith and carpentry included as a subject in the curriculum of the school. However, the condition of traditional handicrafts industry remained static during the colonial period due to lack of finance, competition from cheap industrial products from aboard, lack of government support, inefficient market system lack of training facilities and traditional method of production in Assam. P.K. Dhar rightly observed that "During the pre-independence period, a good number of cottage and village industry were existing in a precarious condition due to lack of finance, market and government patronage."[21] There were certain inherent weakness of the socio-economic system as existed in the medieval times for the decadence of traditional handicrafts during the colonial period in Assam.

2.3. Present Status:

New process has been started for the development of handicrafts with the launching of the First Five Year Plan from 1951 in Assam. Both central and state government has announced various policies for development of handicrafts industry. The All India Handicrafts Board was established in 1952 under the Chairmanship of Ms Kamaladevie Chattopadhyay to study the problems, prospects, preserves and take necessary steps for the development and improvement of the handicrafts in India. For the rapid growth of handicrafts sector in Assam, a broad based programme was undertaken by the state government providing credit, training facilities, technical advice, supply of improved tools and marketing facilities during the planning periods. After independence in 1951, a cottage Industries Training Institute was established at Guwahati to impart training in black-smithy, carpentry, leather works, bamboo and cane works, doll and toy making, potteries, electroplating and electric wiring, gas welding and nail making in the state. The state government has stressed the need to develop the handicrafts industry in order to widen the field of employment and to produce the saleable items so that a self-sustained agrarian economy can be achieved.

In order to develop handicrafts sector, a number of state, regional and central level organizations have been setup in Assam. Some of the organizations which have taken the responsibility of various measures for the growth and development of handicraft are mentioned below.

2.3.1. The Assam Khadi and Village Industries Board (AKVIB):

The AKVI Board was established in 1953 to encourage the development of Khadi and Village industries in the state. The Board has been implementing various programmers for development of khadi and village industries including handicrafts in an organized way with a view to generating rural employment and for upliftment of basic economic structure of rural area of Assam. The Board has also provided of necessary assistance to the artisans for promotion of cane and bamboo industry in Assam.

2.3.2. The Khadi and Village Industries Commission (KVIC):

The KVIC was established in 1957 with headquartered in Mumbai, under Ministry of Industry, Govt. of India. The KVIC has promoted and supported to cane and bamboo works and others 30 major village industries. The KVIC has a separate directorate for cane and bamboo industry. The KVIC works through Khadi and Village Industry Boards in the states. The KVIC has decided to set up a raw material bank for the North Eastern zone. The policy undertaken for strengthening KVIC in the North Eastern zone included introduction especial funding models for rapid implementation of suitable activities in the North Eastern zone. The KVIC is also playing an important role for the expansion and modernization of village industries including cane and bamboo works in the state of Assam.

2.3.3. The Assam Government Marketing Corporation Ltd. (AGMC):

The AGMC was set up in December 1958 with chief objectives of marketing the items of handicrafts and small scale and cottage industries in the state. The AGMC headquarter is situated at Guwahati. The corporation during the last decade dedicated towards the modernization, preservation and patronage of the traditional crafts of the state by encouraging and assisting the master artisans. The AGMC also has taken up different steps to modernize the traditional cane and bamboo in Assam. The corporation has set up sales emporium for the products of cane and bamboo industry within the state as also in metropolitan cities like Delhi and Kolkata. The corporation has been recently transferred to the Sericulture and Weaving Department of Assam.

2.3.4. The Assam Apex Weavers and Artisans Co-Operative Federation Ltd. (ARTFED):

The ARTFED was established in 1977 with headquarter in Guwahati. The ARTFED has been initiating various positive steps to promote wood crafts, cane and bamboo items, bell and brass metal items, decorative textile crafts etc. through regional, national and international markets. It is known that this organization earning profit unlike other government sponsored business organization in the state. The total net profit was 32.46 lakh in the year

2003-2004 in Assam. The organization has set up sales emporium for various handicraft products at different parts of the state. It plays a key role in encouraging the handicrafts artisan in Assam.

2.3.5. The North Eastern Handicrafts and Handloom Development Corporation (NEHHDC):

The NEHHDC was established in 1977 by the Government of India with the main objectives to develop handicrafts and handloom sector in the North Eastern region. The organization provides technical, financial and other support to local master artisans and to promote sales handicrafts items through its own emporium in various places. It has also taken the responsibility for the expansion and market diversification of the cane and bamboo items of Assam and other states of North Eastern region. With the patronage of this corporation, the handicraft products of North Eastern states has been sent around the country and abroad through its emporium, expositions and crafts fairs. The organization has been playing an important role in offering the facility of supply of raw materials, advancing working capital and marketing facilities to handicrafts units including cane and bamboo units in the North East India.

2.3.6. District Industries Center and Commerce (DICC):

The DIC was started from May 1978 at the district level as nodal agency in order to develop village and small industries sector. In nineties the DIC was renamed as DICC. The DICC has been playing a key role in formulating various policies for the benefiting of different types of artisans in the state. The district level organization has extended micro credit support to the artisans in all districts of Assam. The Industrial policy of Assam, 1991 has emphasized the need to strengthen the DICCs in view of the key roles played by these in the growth of various small scale industries and handicrafts units in all districts. As a prime lending district level organization, the role of organization in the future development of the handicrafts sector would be critical in Assam.

2.3.7. The Development Commissioner (Handicrafts):

This central government agency headquarter is situated in Delhi. The DC (H) a Regional Director office for North Eastern region, is situated in Guwahati. The DC (H) set up a development centre for tribal crafts at Jorhat in 1975. On the other hand, a marketing and service extension centre was set up at Gauripur in 1976. The DC (H) gives financial support to the artisans and to hold cane and bamboo exhibitions in different areas like Mumbai, Delhi etc. The financial support is an opportunity for the craftsmen in remote areas to reach large markets and get good returns for their products in Assam. The DC (H) also has been playing an urgent role to develop cane and bamboo handicrafts for best use and generate self employment in the state.

2.3.8. The Assam Small Industries Development Corporation (ASIDC):

The state government categories cane and bamboo units under handicrafts. Therefore they normally come under the purview of department of small and cottage industries in the state. The state government of Assam has set up ASIDC in 1962 with headquarter at Guwahati. The organization is actively engaged in building up small scale industrial units including handicrafts units in Assam. Moreover, the corporation has opened a number of different types of small scale units under its own management and also rendering services for promotion and extension of different schemes such as seed money assistance scheme for the small industries sector in the state. The organization has been playing a positive role to accelerate the process of development and diversification of handicrafts sector in Assam.

2.3.9. The Cane and Bamboo Technology Centre (CBTC):

The CBTC was setup at Guwahati under United Nations Development Programmer (UNDP) scheme in 1999. The United Nations Industrial Development Organization (UNIDO) has formulated projects in order to encourage the cane and bamboo industry in the North-East India. The UNIDO is assigned implementation agency, the North-Eastern Development Finance Corporation Ltd. (NEDIFi) is the field implementation agency and is responsible for project activities carried CBTC. For enough awareness among the people about the prospects of industrial and handicrafts sector utilizing cane and bamboo resources CBTC has organized various workshops and exhibitions in the state.

It is seen that in different areas various type of NGOs have been established for the development of handicrafts in the state. Some NGOs also availed the various assistance from the government for the expansion and modernization of handicrafts industry in the state. It can be noted that NGOs like Crafts Council of Assam, Guwahati, Nalbari District Cane and Bamboo Industry Development Samity, Nalbari, Dhubri Hastashilpa Samabai Samity, Dhubri, Assam Handicrafts Development society, Goalpara and Cane and Bamboo Furniture Co-operative Society, Kokrajhar availed the assistance under the Development Commissioner (Handicrafts), North Eastern region scheme during the 9th plan in Assam. On the national level, the Bamboo Society of

India (BSI), Bangalore, Tata Energy Research Institute (TERI), New Delhi, National Institute of Design (NID), Ahmedabad and Industrial Design Centre, IIT, Mumbai are working to popularizes the cane and bamboo crafts in India. The world-wide organization 'International Network for Bamboo and Rattan' (INBAR) was established in 1997 to provide coordination, leadership and support for research and development of cane and bamboo sector of its member countries including India.

A variety of glorious handicrafts products are made by the artisans of Assam, which are a major useful items sold both at home and abroad. The government of Assam has established sales emporium for the products of cane and

Table 2.1
Exports value of Handicrafts products (Excluding Handmade Carpets) in India
(USA $ Million)

Sl. No	*Years*	*Export value*
1	1998-1999	632.97
2	1999-2000	669.45
3	2000-2001	662.59
4	2001-2002	550.82
5	2002-2003	787.37
6	2003-2004	501.01
7	2004-2005	344.17
Total	-	**4148.38**

Source: CMIE, July, 2005.

bamboo industry in places like Shillong, Kolkota and Delhi in the country. From the state cane and bamboo products are exported to countries like USA, France and Japan. sital-pati from Cachar has captured the market in the Middle East. The handicrafts industry has also become a larger earner of valuable foreign exchange for India. The increasing export value of handicrafts products (excluding handmade carpets) from 1998-99 to 2004-05 in our country as shown Table 2.1

A major feature of the cane and bamboo economy of India as well as Assam is the continuity of utilization of family labour at various stages of production. It is important to note

Table 2.2
Macro Level Performance of Cane and Bamboo Industry in India (In lakh)

Sl. No	*Year/Period*	*Production*	*Sales*	*Employment*
1	4th Plan	105.20	107.11	0.10
2	5th Plan	388.26	443.26	0.66
3	6th Plan	4250.90	5128.85	2.77
4	7th Plan	17744.19	21600.20	6.31
5	1990-91	6950.97	8601.18	1.81
6	1991-92	7639.10	9691.64	1.93
7	1992-93	8972.52	1142.98	2.16
Total	-	**46051.14**	**56997.22**	**15.74**

Source: Mathew, P.M, The Bamboo Economy of Kerala, India: An Analysis of the Production- to- Consumption, System INBAR Working Paper No. 12, New Delhi, 1998.

that the cane and bamboo sector has been playing a major role to providing part-time and full-time employment opportunity for majority of traditional communities in India. The macro level performance of a long period of cane and bamboo industry in India is summarized in Table 2.2

Table-2.2 very clearly reveals that the production, sales and employment opportunity are increased in cane and bamboo sector in our country. It is to be noted that the cane and bamboo products made the largest single contribution in the handicrafts sector in terms of employment in India.

The handicrafts industry occupies an important place in the economy of North Eastern region. The number of

Table 2.3

Number of Craftsmen and Value of Handicrafts Products in the North Eastern Region, 1992-93

Sl. No	*Name of crafts*	*No. of Craftsmen*	*Value (In lakh)*
1.	Artistic Textile	18254	549.9
2.	Brass and Bill Metal	4186	486.7
3.	Cane and Bamboo	20955	952.7
4.	Embrodery	261	14.6
5.	Jewellary	757	32.0
6.	Knitting work	3294	21.9
7.	Sital pati	3625	107.2
8.	Stone carving	519	158.7
9.	Terrakotta/Pottery	29027	217.2
10.	Toys and Dools	94	5.6
11.	Laisamphee	1263	14.0
12.	Wood work	1989	105.5
13.	Painting	21	12.6
14.	Musical Instruments	9	0.8
Total	-	**84254**	**2679.4**

Source: Mali, D.D. and Deka, P, (ed), New Industrial Policy for Village and Small Enterprise, Omsons Publication, New Delhi, 1995.

craftsmen engaged in various handicrafts and the value of Production in respect of handicrafts which are practiced in the North Eastern states during 1991-92 of the region are given in Table 2.3.

From the Table 2.3 it is clear that cane and bamboo, wood work and artistic textile are practiced in all the states of the region. Tripura is very well known for its artistic cane and bamboo crafts in the region as well as in the country. In the recent past the number of artisans and handicrafts units has increased in the North Eastern states. The Table 2.4 gives some idea about the handcrafts artisans and units of the North Eastern region in the year of 2002.

It is interesting to note that in each state, cane and bamboo crafts are practiced as part time and full time occupation by the different types of people of the North Eastern region. For the cane and bamboo crafts resources are available and cane and bamboo are prominent non-timber forest products with immense potential and value for the people of the N-E states. The region is recognized as one of the largest reserve of cane and bamboo.

The climate, culture and raw materials within the region help the cane and bamboo crafts to be spread out all over the North Eastern region. It is also encouraging that some of the artisans of N-E region has received the national award on cane and bamboo crafts. So far 25 artisans from 1967 to 2002 have received the national award on cane and bamboo crafts in the North Eastern states (Appendix IV).

It may be mentioned here that from 1966 to 1998, sixteen craftsmen (Appendix V) have received the Prestigious national award on different crafts for their excellent performances for developing new handicrafts articles. From

Table 2.4

Statewise Handicrafts Artisans and Units in the North Eastern States, 2002

Sl.No	*States*	*No. of Artisans*	*Percentage*	*No. of units*	*Percentage*
1	Arunachal Pradesh,	15735	2.17	4044	2.13
2	Assam	100482	13.85	30360	15.92
3	Manipur	379988	52.39	98051	51.43
4	Meghalaya	53564	7.39	11512	6.04
5	Mizoram	NA	-	NA	-
6	Nagaland	79878	11.01	17603	9.23
7	Tripura	95625	13.19	29072	15.25
Total	-	**725272**	**100.00**	**190642**	**100.00**

Source: NER, Handicrafts at a Glance, Office of the Development Commissioners (Handicrafts), Ministry of Textile, Govt. of India, Guwahati, 2002.

the year 1967 to 1994, ten craftsmen from Assam have received national merit certificates.

Besides national award up to 2000, 8 artisans have received state government award (Appendix VI) on different crafts and 19 artisans have also received state government merit certificate (Appendix VII) in Assam. The master craftsperson who are recipients of national award, merit certificates and state awards, who are more than 60 years of age and whose annual income is below Rs. 1500.00 per annum are eligible for financial grant of Rs. 1000.00 per month every year from office of the Development Commissioner (Handicrafts) in the North Eastern Region. In this connection we may name one famous 48 age old artisan, Dadhi Pathak, Nalbari District of Assam who has made bamboo tooth, bamboo cycle and others excellent of cane and bamboo items.

Over the years, a good number of handicrafts units have been set up in different districts in the state of Assam. It is estimated by DC(H) in Assam total number of handicrafts units were 30,360 and total number of artisans were 1,00,482 in 1995-96. In the Table 2.5 gives the district wise number of handicrafts units and artisans in Assam.

It is seen from Table 2.5 that Kamrup district has highest number of 7904 (26.03%) handicrafts units with 29927(29.78%) artisans and Dhemaji has only 183 (0.60%) number of handicrafts units with 576(0.57%) which is the lowest among all the districts artisans in Assam.

The making of handicrafts product is a subsidiary occupation of the farmers in the rural areas of the state. The rural areas have the highest concentration of handicrafts units in Assam. The total number of handicrafts units and

Table 2.5

District wise Handicrafts Units and Artisans in Assam, 1995-96

Sl. No.	*District*	*No. of Handicraft Units*	*Percentage*	*No. of Handicraft Artisans*	*Percentage*
1	Bongaigaon	293	0.96	927	0.92
2	Barpeta	3915	12.89	14086	14.02
3	Cachar	1041	3.43	2703	2.69
4	Dhubri	1027	3.38	3419	3.40
5	Darrang	833	2.74	2368	2.36
6	Dhemaji	183	0.60	576	0.57
7	Dibrugarh	728	2.40	2736	2.72
8	Goalpara	295	0.97	741	0.74
9	Golaghat	664	2.19	1752	1.74
10	Hailakandi	701	2.31	2951	2.94
11	Jorhat	870	2.87	2645	2.63
12	Kokrajhar	407	1.34	723	0.72
13	Kamrup	7904	26.03	29927	29.78

(Contd.)

(Contd. Table 2.5)

Sl. No.	*District*	*No. of Handicraft Units*	*Percentage*	*No. of Handicraft Artisans*	*Percentage*
14	Karbi-Anglong	657	2.16	1913	1.90
15	Karimganj	1114	3.67	3914	3.90
16	Lakhimpur	1415	4.66	4727	4.71
17	Morigaon	477	1.57	1406	1.40
18	North Cachar Hill	387	1.28	1571	1.56
19	Nagaon	2188	7.21	8575	8.53
20	Nalbari	4068	13.40	8761	8.72
21	Sonitpur	518	1.71	1876	1.87
22	Sivasagar	223	0.74	884	0.88
23	Tinsukia	452	1.49	1301	1.30
Total	-	**30,363**	**100.00**	**1,00482**	**100.00**

Source: Assam, Handicrafts at a Glance, NER, Office of the Development Commisioner (Handicrafts), Ministry of Textile, Govt. of India, Guwahati, 2000.

Table 2.6
Number of Handicrafts Units and Artisans in Assam Classified by Location, 1995-96

Location	*No. of Units*	*Percentage*	*No. of Artisans*	*Percentage*
Rural Areas	28,106	92.57	92,665	92.22
Urban Areas	2,257	7.43	7,817	7.78
Total	**30,363**	**100.00**	**1,00,482**	**100.00**

Source: Assam, Handicrafts at a Glance, NER, Office of the Development Commissioner (Handicrafts), Ministry of Textiles, Govt. of India, Guwahati, 2000.

artisan classified by location in Assam in 1995-96 has been shown in the Table 2.6.

It is known from the Table 2.6 that out of 1, 00,482 artisans 92,665 (92.22%) belonged to the rural areas and the rest numbering 7,817 (7.78%) were from the urban areas.

It is further observed that among the other crafts in terms of production, sales, employment and wages the textile, leather, cane and bamboo, carpentry and blacksmith and village pottery are very common in all areas of the state. The macro level performance of some major crafts in the state is given in Table 2.7.

The Table 2.7 reveals that the village pottery is highly labour intensive than other crafts. The textile workers receive highest wage per worker Rs. 17000.00, where potters get lowest i.e., Rs. 800.00 per worker. The average wage rate for cane and bamboo was Rs. 3000.00 per annum which is considered very nominal to the workers.

Assam being an agricultural state, possesses wide scope for the development of handicrafts. We have already

Table 2.7
Macro Level Performance of Some Major Crafts in Assam, 1999-2000

Sl. No.	*Name of the crafts*	*Value of production (In lakh)*	*Sales (In lakh)*	*No. of Employment*	*Wages (In lakh)*	*Par worker wages (In Rs.)*
1	Textile	6.55	6.01	33	5.58	17000
2	Leather	59.30	67.85	623	35.10	6000
3	Cane and Bamboo	333.65	354.97	5208	143.92	3000
4	Carpentry and Blacksmithy	480.12	560.81	5837	119.51	2000
5	Village Pottery	290.20	262.09	26379	206.09	800
Total	-	**1169.82**	**1251.73**	**38080**	**510.20**	**2000**

Source: Statistical Hand Book, Assam, Directorate of Economics and Statistical, Govt. of Assam, Guwahati, 2001.

mentioned that in order to develop of handicrafts industry, a number of organizations have been set up at the state level, regional level and central level. These organizations are engaged for the promotion and diversification of handicrafts sector in Assam. Moreover, the state government has announced various package of incentives so as to attract more investment and diversification of existing handicrafts industry in Assam. As per provision of the Industrial Policy 1997, a large number of handicrafts units have been benefited from the provision of sales tax exemption and interest subsidy schemes in the state. In the New Industrial Policy 2003, the aim of the government of Assam was to take steps to promote rural handicrafts so as to conserve and enrich cultural heritage, tradition and customs of the state. The budgetary support from state government for the year 1997-98 to 1999-2000 to the handicrafts sector is shown in Table 2.8

The Table 2.8 shows that the budgetary support in Assam increased from Rs. 8.16 lakhs in 1997-98 to Rs. 21.90 lakhs in 1999-2000.

The government of Assam has introduced the relevant economic policy reforms with the rest of the country in 1991. It is observed that after more than one decade the economic reforms it could not create any considerable impact on the development of handicrafts sector in Assam. Considering the high potential of handicrafts sector, the Advisory Committee on Industry 1996, has suggested five short term and three long term measures for development of handicrafts sector in Assam (Appendix-VIII). It is known that the state government has shown less interest for implementation of these suggestions for development of various crafts in the state. During the Eight Five Year Plan about 2610 industrial units in the handicrafts sector were established in Assam,

Table 2.8
Budgetary Support from State Government to the Handicrafts Sector of Assam (In lakh)

Sl. No.	*Sub Head*	*1997-98*	*1998-99*	*1999-2000*
1	Share Capital	-	10.00	10.00
2	Loan (G)	3.00	3.00	5.00
3	Loan (ST)	2.00	2.00	3.00
4	Loan (SC)	3.00	3.00	3.00
Total	-	**8.16**	**18.34**	**21.90**

Source: NER, Handicrafts at a Glance, Office of the Development Commissioner (Handicrafts), Ministry of Textiles, Govt. of India, Guwahati, 2002.

which is as good as nothing. Considering the income and employment potentiality in the handicrafts sector, during the Ninth Five Year Plan, the state government had made up gradation of research and design of handicrafts, exhibitions and fairs schemes, supply of modern tools, supply of finance to handicrafts units, state award to master artisans and others promotional schemes for expansion, diversification and modernization in handicrafts industry in Assam. The basic objective of the Tenth Five Year Plan is to provide adequate infrastructure facilities for setting up handicrafts units and the projected outlay for handicrafts is Rs. 205.00 lakhs in Assam. Accordingly, the Handicrafts Design and Research Centre at Guwahati is to be upgraded by installation of modern tools and machines in collaboration with all India level institutions. The Mukhamantrir Karma Jyoti Ashani is introduced from 2004-05 included the up-liftmen of traditional artisans by financial assistance in the state government of Assam. An amount of Rs. 900.00 lakhs was distributed for implementation of the scheme during 2005-

06. It has also been proposed to give thrust on development of cane and bamboo industries in the Tenth Five Year Plan. Moreover, an amount of Rs. 20.00 lakh is proposed for the Tenth Five Year Plan to award the artisans for their brilliant performance in line with the central government schemes in the state. It is to be noted that an amount of Rs 50 lakh is proposed for Tenth Five Year Plan and Rs. 7.00 lakh for the annual plan 2006-07 for loan to handicrafts artisans Apart from this, it is also proposed to provide budgetary support to ARTFED and AGMC for mobilizing finance from the national level organization, providing raw materials and marketing support to the artisans in the Tenth Five Year Plan of the state. Accordingly a sum of Rs. 50.00 lakh has been earmarked for the purpose in the Tenth Five Year Plan.

Table 2.9 reveals that the handicrafts sector could not achieve its overall targets in the annual plan 2002-03, 2003-04 and 2004-05 of the Tenth Five Year Plan. It is only during the annual plan 2005-06, the handicrafts sector could achieve its targets. The state government has not announced any separate handicrafts policy for modernization and expansion of various crafts after independence.

From the preceding analysis, it is clear that in spite of the heritage, available rich resources of handicrafts and also different measures undertaken by both the central and state government, the handicrafts industry has not been able to develop professionally to an expected level in the state. The artisan in handicrafts sector are mostly in the un-organized sector in Assam. The Directory of Assam Handicrafts revealed that handicrafts has suffered much owing to lack of proper organizations, guidance and encouragement.[22] As a result, handicrafts sector in Assam has failed to show any significant progress due to lack of

Table 2. 9

Year wise Target and Achievement of Handicrafts sector in the Tenth Five Year Plan in Assam (Number)

Items	*2002-03*		*2003-04*		*2004-05*	
	Target	*Achievement*	*Target*	*Achievement*	*Target*	*Achievement*
Loan to Handicrafts artisan	75	25	200	34	200	NIL
Establishment of handicrafts units	2468	2460	2400	2251	2440	2407
Employment Handicrafts	6000	5356	6000	5207	6000	5333
Total	**8543**	**7841**	**8600**	**7492**	**8640**	**7740**

(Contd.)

(Contd. Table 2.9)

2005-06		*2006-07*		*Total*
Target	*Achievement*	*Target*	*Achievement*	
200	200	-	-	934
2440	2440	2440	-	21746
4800	4800	4800	-	48296
7440	**7440**	**7240**	-	**70976**

Source: Draft Annual Plan 2006-07, Vol, II, General Areas Plan, Planning and Development Department, Govt. of Assam, Dispur.

proper infrastructure facilities in the state. There is no separate directorate of handicrafts to look after the development of handicrafts in Assam. The handicrafts organizations like AGMC, ARTFED, KVIB, NEHHDC, the DC (H) etc. are not able to provide basic infrastructural facilities to the handicrafts artisans for the development of handicrafts sector. The handicrafts sector needs financial help, supply of raw materials, market support, training facilities, design guidance, technical knowledge and protection support from stiff competition of other products to create the necessary conditions for Take-off stage for handicrafts sector in Assam. The handicrafts in the state have been facing a number of problems like financial, marketing, modernization, raw material, technical and managerial problems, which have been collectively and severely hampering the development of handicrafts in the state. It is fact that in the present state of affairs of Assam economy artisans are important elements. But they are victims of pervasive anti-poor biases of regional, national and global economic policies for the lack of proper infrastructural facilities in Assam.

There is a scope for improvement of the investment situation in the handicrafts sector in the state which shows that investment friendly climates can be created. In fact, in spite of the problems of development of handicrafts the prospects of this sector is quite bright in the state.

References

1. Bhavnani, Enakshi., *Decorative Designs and Craftsmanship of India*, D.B. Tarporevala Sons and Co. Pvt. Ltd., Bombay, 1982, p. 2.

2. Kosambi, D.D., *The Culture and Civilization of Ancient India in Historical Outline,* Vikas Publishing House Ltd., New Delhi, 1992, p. 195.

3. Abraham, T.M., *Handicrafts in India*, Graphics Columbia, New Delhi, 1964, p. 19.

4. Chandra, Bipan., *The Rise and Growth of Economic Nationalism in India*, People's Publishing House, New Delhi, 1991, p. 55.

5. Quoted by Bhavnani, Enakshi., op. cit., p. 68.

6. Gait, Sri Edward., *A History of Assam*, Lawyer's Book Stall, Guwahati, 1997, p. 22.

7. Guha, Amalendu., "*The Medieval Economy of Assam*," in Raychaudhuri, Tapan and Habib, Irfan (ed.), *The Cambridge Economic History of Indian*, Vol. 1, Cambridge University Press, New Delhi, 1984, p. 489.

8. Borboruah, Hiteeswa., *Ahomar Din*, Publication Board, Assam, Guwahati, 1997, p. 439.

9. Phukan, J.N., "*Products: Agricultural and Non Agricultural*," in Barpujari, H.K. (ed.), *The Comprehensive History of Assam*, Publication Board, Assam, Guwahati, 1994, Vol. 111, p. 118.

10. Nath, D., *History, of the Koch Kingdom, (1515-1615),* Mittal Publications, Delhi, 1989, p. 150.

11. *Assam District Gazetteer*, Lakhimpur District, Govt. of Assam, Guwahati, 1976, p. 220.

12. *Assam State Gazetteer*, Vol. 1, Govt. of Assam, Guwahati, 1999, p. 444.

13. Mali, D.D., *Economic Problems and Planning in Assam*, Omsons Publications, New Delhi, 1989, p. 102.

14. Sarma, S.N., *The New-Vaisnavite Movement and The Satra Institution of Assam*, Guwahati University, Guwahati, 1966, p. 174.

15. Baruah, S.L., *A Comprehensive History of Assam*, Munshiram Manoharlal Publishers Pvt. Ltd., New Delhi, 1985, p. 438.

16. Quoted by Sarma, Satyendranath, In *A Socio-Economic and Cultural History of Medieval Assam,* Guwahati, 1989, p. 306.

17. Barpujari, H.K., *Assam in the Days of the Company*, NEHU Publications, Shillong, 1996, p. 259.

18. Saikia, Rajen., *Social and Economic History of Assam, 1853-1921*, Manohar, New Delhi, 2000, p. 56.

19. Barpujari, H.K. (ed.), *The Comprehensive History of Assam*, Vol. V, Publication Board, Assam, Guwahati, 1993, p. 101.

20. Ibid, 105.

21. Dhar, P.K., *The Economy of Assam*, Kalyani Publishers, New Delhi, 1998, p. 103.

22. *Directory of Assam Handicrafts*, Directorate of Industries, Govt. of Assam, Guwahati, 1978, p. 1.

3

Review of Existing Literature on Handicrafts

There was dearth of literature on handicrafts in Assam up to the seventies of the last century. But, in recent time, interests in handicrafts are shown by some writers, researchers and government agencies in the state. Our research work is an humble beginning and attempts to analyses the handicrafts in Assam with particular reference to cane and bamboo works. In this chapter we intend to provide a review of such literature, like research studies, survey reports and some important relevant works on handicrafts in India as well as in Assam. It may be mentioned that constituents of N.E. Region are once a part of Assam and in any historical study Assam cannot be singled out from other part of N.E. Region.

Verrier Elwin[1] was the first writer who wrote about the handicrafts in N-E region systematically far back in 1959. In his study, Elwin attempted to discuss the various traditional crafts of Arunachal Pradesh which was a part of Assam. In his work the author has pointed out the traditional crafts which affects on dress and personal adornment of the people of the state. The author observed that the best Adis cane works are seen in the making of varieties of artistically design hats. The author also expressed the view that studying technique, design then with caution, humility and patience help the tribal artisans to select the excellent models of their own rich traditional for preservation and development modern techniques and styles out of their past glorious heritage.

T.A. Abraham works on "Handicrafts in India,"[2] is considered to be one of the important study on this subject. In this work, the author systematically studied the decline and survival of handicrafts. He opines that in ancient days, there were powerful guilds in almost all fields of crafts, like pottery, metal ware, store work, basket making. In the discussion of the role of handicrafts in the country, the author expressed the view that crafts in every home means economic stability of the country. He has rightly admitted that there is a good lot that we can profitably learn from the two crafts countries, Japan and Switzerland in the development of handicrafts.

S.N. Sarma, in his study on "The New-Vaisnative Movement and The Satra Institutions of Assam,"[3] examined the role of satra institutions in the development of various crafts in Assam. According to the author, some person were engaged for the creation of various crafts for the use in daily life of the people living in the satra. Some wooden, cane and bamboo works, such as blankets (thanga), rush, mate and mattress (kath, pati and dhara), have been used in all the satras. He also mentioned that the celibate bhaktas, in their off time engaged themselves in such crafts in the satra.

In an another study S.N. Sarma[4] expressed the view that indigenous crafts had undergone changes in motifs, designs and technique from time to time as a rest of the infusion of blood from new elements of production. He mentioned that the fishing implements, spinning and weaving implements, ploughing implements and various households implements were made form cane and bamboo. The author rightly observed that the medieval crafts of Assam must be considered as making a new phase in the history of cultural development in Assam.

Radhakamal Mukerjee[5] reviews history of the economic condition of the artisans between 1600 to 1800 in India. The author is of the opinion that due to immoderate price of the raw materials as well as the burden of several kinds of taxes levied on the artisans and their products, it drove them into the clutches of the intermediator and the financers of India. The artisans could not overcome the problems which left the artisans altogether destitute in the country. The author also mentioned that the market of the handicrafts was chiefly confined to the limited class of the Mughal aristocracy in India. In that time there was small scope of expansion for this class of crafts and the Mughal nobility often preferred variety of new foreign products in India.

In the Sivasagar District Gazetteer[6] it was recorded that making of cane and bamboo items are pursued by the rural family especially agriculturists in the Sivasagar district of Assam during the sixties. The rural family makes cane and bamboo articles for their domestic requirement; but some important products are sold in the local market. The Gazetteer also mentioned that the cane and bamboo industry, making common hat (japi) is one of the most indispensable products in the scanty paraphernalia of the open air workers, especially cultivators and tea garden workers of the district. The manufacture of typical design cane furniture calls for a high degree of skill on the part of the artisans. The Gazetteer reveled that various crafts like pottery, carpentry, jewellery, metal works are of great prospects for development of the district.

Another gazetteer the Darrang District Gazetteer[7] recorded that like other traditional crafts, the cane and bamboo works earned wide appreciation in pre British period of Assam. Every family made at least a part of its home requirements of cane and bamboo items. The cane and bamboo craft is mainly a household industry and it provides full-time occupation of the skilled artisans who produce artistic decorative baskets, furniture and mats on commercial scale of the district. The Gazetteer mentioned that the cane and bamboo works are generally carried out by the male members of the family taking part predominately in the rural areas in their spare time as a subsidiary occupation in the district. The Gazetteer also noted that due to high demand for cane and bamboo products and the availability of necessary raw materials, there is considerable potential for development of cane and bamboo crafts on commercial basis in the Darrang district of Assam, in present day times.

Alemchiba[8] has described the various rich traditional handicrafts of Nagaland. In this work the author pointed out the different mischievous forces playing their parts against the rich traditional handicrafts and also how the craftsmen had their pride in mind of their own products. He mentioned that the Nagas are expert in the making of various shapes and sizes of baskets for their own domestic use. The raw materials used for baskets are the cane and bamboo found plentifully in the state. In their leisure time from the normal economic pursuits the Nagas are engaged in bamboo works in the state. The author mentioned that security of the village, thick jungles and deep rivers have created problems for producing large quantity of handicrafts for business purposes. The author opines that machine made products and the sense of inferiority in the face of the commercial products of civilization are others unfavorable factors for the development of traditional handicrafts in the state.

B.K. Barua[9] has studied the ancient crafts system of Assam. He observed that the craftsmen like weavers, spinners, goldsmiths, potters and workers in ivory, wood, cane and bamboo, played a dominant role in day to day life of the people in ancient Assam. The people of the state always gave special attention for bamboo plantation in the fact that bamboo used for building house, bridges, making baskets, traps for fishing and hunting, cooking utensils and musical instrument of the people. Artistic designs of cool mats (sital patis) were made and these mats were generally used by the rich people. The author referred that mat making is an important craft in Assam.

A comparative study on the crafts of India and Pakistan's by Swarup[10] discussed the various aspects of India and Pakistan crafts during the last five thousand years, of the two countries. By reviewing the artistic heritage of Indian crafts the author expressed the view that Indian crafts are an expression of Indian civilization as a whole from ancient time down to the present day.

M .N. Upadhyay[11] has made an attempt to an economic analysis of the handicrafts industry in the state of Andhra Pradesh in 1973. This study provides a historical back-drop to the handicrafts and traces its development since the Vedic times in India. The author also discussed about technology, designs, quality control, marketing and export promotion of the handicrafts industry of the state as well as of the country. The study has thrown light on the factors affecting the growth of productivity and suggests measures to develop the handicrafts industry of Andhra Pradesh .The economic concepts like dualism, saving effect, sectoral analysis and the Cobb-Douglas Production function have been used in analyzing the growth and development of handicrafts industry of the country.

S.R.Sharma[12] examined the causes of decline of Indian handicrafts during the British period from 1857 to 1947 in India. He observed that with the advent of the British Raj the disappearance of the local courts of Rajas and Nawbs had contributed to the decline of rich traditional handicrafts in India. In his study the author shows that in the old economic structure of India the self-sufficient village held a place of pride and the country artisans were forming an important factor to the population swing in the villages of India. By examining the handicrafts sector, the author expressed the view that the expansion of railway services helped the replacement of home made items by foreign goods and facilitated the exports of raw materials.

M.K.Pal[13] has made an attempt at a comprehensive study of the traditional crafts such as pottery, terrocotta, wood-carving, ivory-carving, stone-carving, jewellery, textile and image-making in the country. In his work, the author examined the tribal crafts and craftsmen and opined that the different types of utilitarian, decorative and ritual products are made by the tribal people, which not only serve the needs of the common people, but also satisfy the artistic tastes of the sophisticated communities in India. The author also discussed the socio-economic life of the artisans with special reference to their social and economic status of the society. He also studied the origin and development of the different crafts and the role of the crafts and craftsmen with the various crafts-institutions connected with the development of the different crafts in the country.

The Directorate of Industries was published a Directory of Assam Handicrafts in 1978[14]. According to the directory, lack of proper organization, guidance and encouragement are the major problems of the declining artistic heritage and tradition of the bamboo crafts in the state. In spite of abundance of raw materials which is considered to be a contributory factor for the development of cane crafts in every district of Assam, the cane industry also has suffered much owing to lack of organization and encouragement to the artisans in the state.

In his work on "Tribal Art and craft,"[15] A.K. Das has made an attempt to assess the relative position about an ancient craft of basketry in the society, economy and culture in the tribes of Arunachal Pradesh. The varied use of cane and bamboo and the variety of baskets is also reflected in the social, political and economic life of all the tribes. The author mentioned that baskets and similar other products made of basketry technique, used a religious paraphernalia, are found among all the tribes of the state. Basketry works have created a cultural environment of the traditional industry in Arunachal Pradesh.

Bhattacharya[16] has made an attempt to examine the nature of problems faced by the rural artisans and the role played by the government in removing these problems in the country. The study has thrown light on the factors affecting the growth and development of the rural industries to deliver the products in proper time and place in different parts of the country. The author revealed that rural artisan activity generally depends on local resources which are utilized by his traditional tools, equipments, skill and help of his family members for items production. The rural artisan have been playing a very important role in supplying various artistic and common items for rural development in the country. The author opines that there is a need of strong policy support to the rural artisans from unfair competition of the rival organized sector. This work has also highlighted the rural artisans programme which can be operated to create capacity as well as income creating among the artisans in our country.

Another pioneering work on handicrafts is that of J. Dhamaja[17] who has made a scholarly study on the gradual development of handicrafts, role and importance of handicrafts in day to day life of the people of India. According to the author, India's handicrafts reached a very high point of perfection during the Moghul period. After the British Raj in India, the machine made goods began to compete with the items of Indian handicrafts products. This led to the gradual decline of Indian handicrafts. She also observed that the prevalence of various crafts in the country reflects its heritage in religion, social, customs and beliefs.

The Small Industry Extension Training Institute conducted a survey[18] handicrafts in Assam 1982. According to the survey, shortage of raw materials, low production capacity, lack of finance, competition with the products of other states, lack of new designs and the peculiar topographical features are the problems faced by the handicrafts artisans in Assam. The survey report observed that the cane and bamboo crafts are still taken as a subsidiary occupation along with farming in the state. The crafts are still in the traditional stages and they are cornered by all types of problems. The survey report mentioned that due to abundant raw material sources and the adoption of life style of the people, cane and bamboo craft is perhaps the most universal of all the crafts practiced in Assam.

R.D. Gupta's[19] work deals with the studying the crafts of medieval Assam with keeping in view the various ethnic elements of its making. In this work the author has shown that different crafts like pottery, terracotta, wood, ivory, bamboo work, metal ware and jewelry had played various positive role among the deferent ethnic groups of art, cultural and economic life development of the society. By reviewing the heritage of medieval crafts the author also opines that the different crafts were an expression of varied modes, nobility and beauty of medieval Assam.

Aditi Shirali's work on "Textile and bamboo craft of the North Eastern Region,"[20] has emphasized the close economic and cultural bond between various crafts and the everyday life and agrarian economy of the North Eastern states. By studying the market structure, the author expressed the view that in the plains areas of Assam, Tripura and Manipur the weekly hat (Market) gives one the opportunity of selling cane and bamboo baskets, reed mats, sithol pati mats, fish traps, all kinds of agricultural implements and weaving accessories.

Amalendu Guha, in his work on "The Medieval Economy of Assam,"[21] observed that during the medieval period of Assam, the Kalita caste formed diverse occupational groups such as potters, blacksmiths, goldsmiths, bell-metal artisans, carpenters, boat builders and weavers. By examining the craft and technology system in the medieval period of Assam, he expressed the view that the uneven development of technology over a range of craft was due to availability of raw materials. Simple bamboo and wooden implements were used in most of the crafts at that time. As a result, manual skill was raised to a elevated level of perfection to achieve the desired ends during the medieval period of Assam.

The work on "Modernization of Production Process of Handicrafts,"[22] T. Sankaranarayanan has made an attempt to study the role of traditional handicrafts industry on the economy of North-East India. He observed that the handicrafts industry needs succor for its revival. This industry is threatened by stiff competition from the highly organized manufacturing industries. Considering the problems faced in the handicrafts industry in the North-East India, he has emphasized the need for modernization of production process of handicrafts.

Gunnar Myrdal[23] has expressed the view that the crafts have deep and well-established roots of economic environment in South Asia. The artisan suffered a harsher fate during the colonial period in India than did their counterparts elsewhere in South Asian countries. Myrdal rightly observed that the successful agricultural policy is a necessary element for the development of village crafts and the demand for the articles of village artisans depends in big part, on the levels of income in agricultural sector. In the case of India the author noted that the production of spinning and weaving crafts increased very substantially during the first part of planning period in the country.

Probin Kumar Sarma[24] has made an attempt to discus the role of cane and bamboo resources in the economic development of Assam. Among the great variety of handicrafts units, cane and bamboo units have been playing a vital role in providing employment to a considerable number of people in Assam. The cane and bamboo works depend on the forest resources which exist in many parts of the state. He assessed that substantial amount of income including valuable foreign resources are earned by the craftsmen in the state by selling and exporting the items of these handicrafts units.

The study, "Genetic Diversity and Socio-Economic importance of Bamboo in India,"[25] undertaken by Thomas, Arora and Singh have discussed the role of bamboo resources in socio-economic system of India. They noted that bamboo serves both the poor and the rich people with its large number of useful products and these resources are renewable source of energy in the form of fuel for the rural people in India. Articles like mats, basketries, ropes, beds, bridges, umbrella handles, pipes, fans, brushes, nails, anchors, fishing, rods, furniture poles and agricultural implements are made from bamboo commonly used of the people in the country. They also mentioned that it is unavoidably need to check devastation and protect natural vegetation of bamboo and to increase bamboo cultivation for meeting the increasing demand in India.

Sarbeswar Rajguru's work[26] is an important publication throwing light on the various crafts during the medieval period of Assam. In this work, the author discussed the wooden works, cane and bamboo works, crafts on animal products, stone works, pottery, working on metal, gold, silver, copper, bell-metal and brass work in the medieval period. In his discussion on cane and bamboo works, he said that cane and bamboo were mainly used for the construction of house, various kinds of fishing instruments, weaving instruments, utensils and instruments used in the daily life of the Assamese people. A large number of artistic household cane and bamboo articles are listed by the author in his work.

In the discussion of handicrafts in Assam, P.C.Goswami[27] noted that bamboo works, black-smithy, pottery and carpentry are important occupation practiced in various place and giving employment opportunity to the people of Assam. The author mentioned that Sarthebari, Hajo, Titabar and Raha are important centres for manufacture of hand-made bell-metal wares in the state. Barpeta is an important place for manufacture of attractive ivory products of Assam. The author also suggested that cane and bamboo works may be developed on small-scale in the state.

Sanjay Kathuria's[28] work is concerned with the analysis of government policy for development of handicrafts and problems and prospects of handicrafts exports in the country. He expressed the view that the handicrafts sector is not only helping to redistribute income among the poor but also helping foreign exchange earning for the country. The comparative advantage of India in handicrafts production could be used to capitalize in favorable exports trends in the global economy. In the discussion on handicrafts exports the author remarks that in India export problem appears to be largely a production and organization problems. The author also mentioned that if the right environment is created at home, than Indian handicrafts could also flourish and demand of handicrafts products will automatically increase in the foreign market in the world.

The study on "Economic Problems and Planning in Assam,"[29] undertaken by D.D Mali, has discussed the present status of handicrafts through a planned process in Assam. The author observed that among the important handicrafts, cane and bamboo work is a predominant vocation in the state. This craft is the most widely practiced due to the skill of the people and the availability of raw materials in Assam. He also mentioned that finance, marketing and raw materials are the major problems faced by the handicrafts artisans in the state.

P.C. Dutta[30] studied variety of crafts including weaving, carpet making, wood craving, cane and bamboo works, ornament making, paper making, smithy work, pottery and ivory work practices the people of Aurnachal Pradesh. In this study the author mentioned that the people have a tradition of artistic craftsmanship which manifests itself through their variety of handicrafts products of the state. Cane and bamboo work is of a very high standard and most of the domestic requirements are made of cane and bamboo in the state. The author expressed the view that mass production and infusion of new elements in the crafts have not added much to the cause of revival of these traditional crafts. The author opines that the revival of traditional crafts should be realistic because crafts belong to the people and survive on their patronage and good will.

Milton S. Sangma studies, "Crafts and Technology of the Garos,"[31] and observed that the Garos have evolved certain cultural traits and developed distinct crafts and technology of their own through some of the weapons, dresses and ornaments in Meghalaya. The author opines that the Garos are specialized in the various crafts and the crafts have utility in the day to day life of the Garos. In this study, the author mentioned that one cannot imagine the Garos' simple traditional life without the crafts in Meghalay

Among the works which have laid special emphasis on the cane and bamboo crafts, that of Mutua Bahadur is mentionable[32]. He has made the analytical study of history, culture, preparation technique of cane and bamboo products and its impact on socio-economic development of hills in valley of Manipur. By studying in details the existing cane and bamboo craft system in the state, he observed that the indigenous technique takes less time and offers a more efficient job than the usual method of splitting bamboo.

In his work on "Bamboo Craft in Integrated tribal Development"[33] P.S. Mukharjee wants to focus bamboo as a part of integral development of village in India. Though bamboo grows widely in the country, very little efforts have been made to grow it commercially. He also observed that the involvement of BAIF's (Bharatiya Industries Foundation) in bamboo relative activities which have taken up a number of programmers related to bamboo throughout the country a good beginning in this regard is being made.

Kamaladevi Chattopadhyay[34] has analyzed the whole gamut of crafts and in relation to historical, cultural, economical and sociological evolution the centuries of men in the country. She opines that handicrafts have been the very fundamental activities of human society in their day to day life. She also examined the variety of Indian handicrafts and emphasized the need for development of richness of Indian handicrafts for socio-economic and cultural benefits of the people in India.

An important study on the handicrafts of North-East India has been done by Satyendra Narayana Chowdhury.[35] He expressed the view that though cane and bamboo is common everywhere in the North-East India, the role of these resources in the economic development is insignificant.

He reveled that cane and bamboo products have utility in day to day life of the people of North Eastern region. The author also discussed the role of the AGMC, NEHHDC, the KVIC and the Khaid Board for the development of various crafts in the North-East India.

The Advisory Committee on Industry of Assam[36] reviewed the handicrafts sector in Assam. The committee has suggested eight measures for the development of handicrafts in the state. The committee suggested that the government should promote the private sector in Assam to operate a mechanism for availability of raw materials for the artisans. The development of marketing infrastructural scheme, entrepreneurial skill development, provision of financial support and other information should be introduced for the development of handicrafts in Assam.

In his work "Design Inputs into Craft Areas: Implications for Rural Development and Employment Generation,"[37] A.G. Rao has emphasized the need of bamboo craft recognize as an industrial activity to achieve a higher level of commerce and the consequent employment generation in trade and production. In this work the author opines that a fresh approach to craft is necessary to recognized craft as an industrial activity and a means to develop creativity in general education in developing countries. Bamboo craft has been pursued as a folk craft in most of the bamboo growing developing countries. He remarks that folk crafts which catered to the needs of the rural population have remained simple and produce of folk crafts excelled in harmonious social settings. The author also emphasized the need of creation of a marketing agency for bamboo crafts and also said that marketing is most important for the financially hard pressed of bamboo artisans.

P.M. Mathew[38] has described the economic possibilities and potential of the cane and bamboo industry in the context of South and South-East Asia. He opines that the development of cane and bamboo sector needs to be looked into at level of analysis of issues and the formation of appropriate development politics. In this study the author said that the productivity, resources and employment studies are the major thrust of studies on cane and bamboo sector in South and South-Eats Asia. The cane and bamboo activity are largely based on the mainstay of poverty groups in South and South-East Asia. The author suggested that a balanced approach is needed for growth, distribution and examine the cane and bamboo sector in the context of the emerging changes in the overall business environment as well as in the global economy as a whole.

In an another study P.M. Mathew[39] focused on the institutional aspects of bamboo production to consumption system of Kerala. The author used the term production-to-consumption system which refers to the entire chain of activities from productions of raw materials through various stages of intermediate sales and processes to final consumption level. In this work the author observed that a major feature of the bamboo economy is the continuity of utilization of family labour a different stages of bamboo extraction and consumption for the reason of the bamboo enterprises are basically cottage level in Kerala. The sickness among existing bamboo units are man problems in the bamboo industry in the state. The author suggested that a series of studies on the bamboo material utilization pattern in various bamboo productlines as well as among different clusters are necessary for the development of bamboo industry in Kerala.

In his work "The Global Environment Debate: The Role of Bamboo,"[40] Salleh Mohd. Nor has made a modest attempt to explores the role of bamboo as an eco-friendly material in regarding environment problems. He expressed the view that the history of bamboo is inextricably interwoven with human history in Asia. Bamboo is an environment friendly resource that it can play an important role in soil conversation. The author opines that generation of new knowledge and application of science and technology will help in the preservation and use of eco-friendly bamboo resources, which will help sustainable development of the human society.

Kanwarjit[41] has conducted a study on the place of bamboo crafts in the life of tribal communities in the Karjat region of the Weastern Ghats in Maharashtra. The author opines that the region has a live tradition of bamboo crafts, the bamboo work is seasonal and the younger generation does not seem attracted to bamboo crafts. In his study the author observes that there in immense scope for bamboo related development activities in the Karjat region of the Weastern Ghats in Maharashtra.

P.K. Haldar[42] has discussed the problems of marketing development of handicrafts in the state of Tipura. In this work the author opines that the market and marketing forces determines items, distribution and profit. The lack of infrastructural network and land lock situation stands in the way of development of marketing of handicrafts in the state. The author has suggested that facilities and support for development of marketing be extended to the individual or organization of those who have associated in operation and contribution in the field of promotion of marketing of handicrafts in the state.

The Ministry of Environment and Forest, Government of India, has published an important and useful work in the field of handicrafts in India[43]. This work covers a detailed discussion and examination of the cane and bamboo sector of the country. This report expressed the view that cane and bamboo holds a potential for setting, large number of small and medium industry at low capital investment, producting numerous items. This report also provides a descriptive account of various institution created by the central and state government for the development of cane and bamboo sector and bamboo artisans welfare in the country. This report also noted that cane and bamboo are put together in the same category in the government terminology. Cane constitutes an integral part of the tropical forest eco-system in India.

The Assam State Gazetteer[44] is an important source of official literature on handicrafts in Assam. This Gazetteer covers various crafts practiced by the people of Assam. On cane and bamboo crafts, the gazetteer mentioned that the cane and bamboo industry provides a full time occupation to the highly skilled artisans who produce only fine decorative baskets, furniture and mats on commercial scale in the state. The potentiality of making cane and bamboo items on commercial scale is quite considerable in Assam. According to this gazetteer, the death of skilled workers or technical guidance has limited scope for development of cane and bamboo industry to a great extern in the state.

D.N. Dhar[45] has attempted to discuss on Kashmir artisans from ancient to modern times on the basis of evidence and real reference. In this work the author observed that the inspiration of the artisans have mainly come from the rich natural environment of the valley of Kashmir. In the state, so many beautifully design items produced by artisans for common use of the people. In his discussion on the artisans of the Paradise the author expressed the view that the taxation policy is not favorable for the artisans, which pauperized the artisans of Kashmir. The author also mentioned that the artisans of Kashmir produced such pieces of valuable art as were adored and praised by the art lovers throughout the world.

An important non-official work on handicrafts is provided by the Assam Prakalap.[46] The report of Asom Prakalap observed that handicrafts are important area, which if exploited to the fullest, potential may bring prosperity to the economic health of the economy of Assam. In the context of craft system of Assam, the report mentioned that the artisans of Assam, created wonderful item on crafts like sarap, dunars, flower vase from brass were and bell-metal, cane and bamboo furnitures decorative terracotta items, ivory items, sitalpati with exquisite design. According to the report, limited raw material sources, unorganized productions base, limited market opportunities, lack of modernization efforts, lack of proper guidance and encouragement, limited credit facilities, high production cost, stiff competition from outside and lack of exposures are the major reasons for low productivity and performance of handicrafts industry in Assam. Reviewing the handicrafts industry in Assam, the report reasonably expressed the view that for the development of handicrafts sector we have the required skills and talents, we have the necessary and proper guidance, help and country-operation particularly on quality up-gradation, finance and marketing from concerned departments, organizations, institutions and professionals of the state.

Saikia[47] has discussed and described the decline of handicrafts during the British period from 1853 to 1921 in

Assam. In his study the author opines that some crafts which so long satisfied the needs of the people started declining with the opening of free trade with Bengal during nineteenth century. Though wood carving and ivory carving were two famous crafts at that time, due to small number of people engaged in the works and products bring limited, the crafts had no chance of turning in to an industry. In the discussion of iron production the author noted that the iron making was not extensive but it was an important industry during the Ahom Period in Assam. Reviewing the domestic crafts scenario the author remarked that basketry and making of various implements of daily use like box, container, comb, hand-fan, umbrella, mats, agricultural, gardening, marketing and measuring tools, writing and painting, some musical instruments, fish-cashing equipments and cooking implements survived at that period in Assam.

Gopalkrishnan's work[48] is a notable contribution in understanding the handicrafts in Assam. In this fair analysis the author mentioned that cane and bamboo, brass metal, bell-metal industry, sital pati, wood carving, kuhilla koth, ivory work, solapith, pottery, doll making, toy making, jewellery and stone carving have been playing an important role, particularly providing alternative occupation to rural population in Assam. The author identified that finance, marketing and raw materials are major problems faced by the handicrafts units of Assam. In reviewing the present problems, he also said that there is lack of training and scientific management in handicrafts industry in Assam. The author also emphasized the need of development of various important crafts for social, cultural and economic up liftmen in the state.

Another important study on crafts production has been done by Liebl and Ray[49] who have given an overview of crafts production and marketing system in the country. They examined why the potential has not so far been extended and realized in India. They mentioned that the vastly potential remain underutilized and give the myriad problems on both demand and supply side of the country. The rapid globalization has brought the handicrafts face to face with a unique set of challenges in India. They opined that for crafts development long term steps need to be taken to establish positive brand image in the domestic and international markets. In the discussion of problems specific to traders and exporters they noted that there is need for comprehensive and coordinated policy for the overall improving of the lives of artisans and who conduct their enterprises with integrity and dedication in India.

Last but not the least important work to be mentioned in this connection is the key note address at a national level seminar on "Present Status of Handicrafts in the North-Eastern Region" by K.C. Borah.[50] Borah observed that the handicrafts are famous for their artistic creativity, exquisite design and superb workmanship, which reflect the cultural values of the N-E region. He opines that inadequacy of finance, absence of trained personal, unorganized marketing system, stiff competition from the organized industrial products, non availability of raw materials and poor consumer demand of the N-E region are the common problems for handicrafts sector. In spite of various constrains that are faced by the handicrafts sector it has good prospects for development through diversification of products and modernization process. The handicrafts units can provide employment and income opportunities to large number of people as these units are mostly labour intensive. In the discussion of future prospects of handicrafts sector in the context of present liberalized economy, he mentioned that if proper training facilities, financial support, market information, input supply and other infrastructural facilities are provided adequately, craft products of N-E states will certainly be able to compete in the global market.

References:

1. Elwin, Verrier., *The Art of the North-East Frontier of India*, North East Frontier Agency, Shillong, 1959.

2. Abraham, T.M., *Handicrafts in India*, Guphies Columbia, New Delhi, 1964.

3. Sarma, S.N., *The New-Vaisnavite Movement and the Satra Institutions of Assam*, Guwahati University, Guwahati, 1966.

4. Sarma, S.N., *A Socio-Economic and Cultural History of Assam*, Guwahati, 1989.

5. Mukerjee, Radhakamal., *The Economic History of India, 1600-1800*, Kitab Mahal, Allahbad, 1967.

6. *Assam District Gazetteer, Sivasagar District*, Govt. of Assam Shillong, 1967.

7. *Assam District Gazetteer, Darrang District*, Govt. of Assam, Guwahati, 1978

8. Alemchiba, M., *The Arts and Crafts of Nagaland*, Naga Institute of culture, Govt. of Nagaland, Kohima, 1968.

9. Barua, B.K., *A Cultural History of Assam*, Vol. I, Lawyer's Book Stall, Guwahati, 1969

10. Swarup, Shanti., *5000 Years of Arts and Crafts in India and Pakistan*, D.B. Traporevals Sons and Co-private Ltd., Mumbai, 1969.

11. Upadhyay, M.N., *Economics of Handicrafts Industry*, S. Chand and Co.-(pvt) Ltd., New Delhi, 1973.

12. Sharma, S.R., "*Cottage Industries: 1857-1947*," in Singh, V.B (ed.), *Economic History of India (1857-1956)*, Allied Publishers Limited, New Delhi, 1975.

13. Pal, M.K., *Crafts and Craftsmen in Traditional India*, Kanak Publications, New Delhi, 1978.

14. *Directory of Assam Handicrafts*, Directorate of Industries, Govt. of Assam, Guwahati, 1978.

15. Das, A.K., *Tribal Art and craft*, Agam Kala Prakashan, Delhi, 1979.

16. Bhattacharya, Sib Nath., *Rural Industrialization in India (Its Nature and problems)*, B.R. Publishing corporation, Delhi, 1980.

17. Dhamaja, J., *India Folk Arts and Crafts*, National Book Trast, India, New Delhi, 1981.

18. *Assam Handicraft Survey,* Small Industry Extension Training Institute, Guwahati, 1982.

19. Gupta, R.D., *Art of Medieval Assam,* Cosom Publications New Delhi, 1982.

20. Shirali, Aditi., *Textile and Bamboo Crafts of the North Eastern Region*, National Institute of Design, Ahmedabad,1983.

21. Guha, Amalendu., "*The Medieval Economy of Assam*," in Raychaudhuri, Tapan and Habib, Infan (ed.), *The Cambridge Economic Histoty of India*, Vol. I, Combridge University Press, New Delhi, 1984.

22. Sankaranarayanan, T., "*Modernization of Production Process of Handicrafts*," in Ganguly, J.B (ed.), *Marketing in North-East India*, Omsons Publication, Guwahati, 1984.

23. Myrdal, Gunnar, *Asian Darma*, Vol. II , Kalyani Publishers, New Delhi, 1985.

24. Sarma, Probin Kumar, *Role of Forest Resources on the Economy of Assam*, Unpublished Ph. D thesis, Dibrugarh University, Dibrugarh, 1986.

25. Thomas, T.A., Arora, R.K and Singh, Ranbir, "*Genetic Diversity and Socio-Economic importance of Bamboos in India*," in Rao, A.N., Dhabarajan, G and Sastry, C. B (ed.), *Recent Research on Bamboo*, Proceeding of the International Bamboo worker shop, 6-14 October 1985, Hangzhou, The Chinese Academy of Forestry, People's Republic of China, 1997.

26. Rajguru, Sarbeswar, *Medieval Assamese Society, 1228-1826*, Nagaon, 1988

27. Goswami, P.C., *The Economic Development of Assam*, Kalyani Publishers,New Delhi, 1988 .

28. Kathuria, Sanjay, *Indian Handicraft Exports, Constraints and Prospects*, Tata MaGraw-Hill Publishing Company Limited,New Delhi, 1988

29. Mali, D.D., *Economic Problems and Planning in Assam*, Omsons Publications, New Delhi, 1989.

30. Dutta, P.C., "*Handicrafts of Arunachal Pradesh*," in Dutta, P.C and Duarah, D.K (ed.), *Handicrafts of Arunachal Pradesh*, Directorate of Research, Govt. of Arunchal Pradesh, Itanagar, 1990.

31. Sangma, Milton S., "*Crafts and Technology of the Garos*," in Singh, Jai Prakash and Sengupta, Gautam, *Archaeology of North-Eastern India*, Vikas Publishing House Pvt Ltd., New Delhi, 1991.

32. Bahadur, Mutura., *Cane And Bamboo Craft of Manipur*, Mutur Museum, Imphal, 1994.

33. Mukharjee, P.S., "*Bamboo Craft in Integrated Tribal Development*," in Rao, A.G and Koli, Madhavi (ed.), *Bamboo Craft Design*, Industrial Design Center, IIT, Mumbai, 1994.

34. Chattopadhyay, Kamaladevi., *Handicrafts of India*, Indian Council for Cultural Relations, New Delhi, 1995.

35. Chowdhury, Satyendra Narayan., *India's North East Industrial Resources and Opportunities*, Dibrugarh, 1996.

36. *Report of Advisory Committee on Industry*, Vol. I, Assam, 1996.

37. Rao, A.G., "*Design Inputs into Crafts Areas: Implications for Rural Development and Employment Generation,*" in Rao, Ramanuja. I.V and Sastry, Cheral. B (ed.), *Bamboo, People and the Environment,* Proceeding of the 5th International Bamboo Workshop and the Iv International Bamboo Congress, Ubud, Bali, Indonesia, 19-22 June 1995, Vol. 3, Engineering and Utilization, International Development Research Centre, Canada, 1996.

38. Mathew, P.M., "*Towards a New Approach to Understanding the Bamboo Economy,*" in Rao, Ramanuja. I.V. and Sastry, Cherla. B (ed.), *Bamboo people and the Environment*, Proceeding of the Vth International Bamboo Workshop and the Iv International Bamboo Congress, Ubud, Bali, Indonesia, 19-22 June 1995, Vol. 4, Socio Economic and Culture, International Development Research Centre, 1996.

39. Mathew, P.M., *The Bamboo Economy of Kerala, India: An Analysis of the Production-to-Consumption Systems.* INBAR Working Paper No. 12, International Network for Bamboo and Rattan, New Delhi, 1998.

40. Nor, Salleh. Mohd., *"The Global Environmental Debate: The Role of Bamboo,"* in Rao, Ramanuja. I.V and Sastry, B (ed.), *Bamboo, People and the Environment.*, Proceeding of the Vth International Bamboo Workshop and the IV International Bamboo Congress, Ubud, Bali, Indonesia, 19-22 June 1995, Vol. I, Propagation and Management, International Development Research Centre, 1996.

41. Nagi, Kanwarjit., *The Status of Bamboo and Bamboo Craft in Karjat, India, and Strategies for Development,* INBAR Working Paper No. 19, International Network for Bamboo and Rattan, New Delhi, 1998.

42. Haldar, P.K., Facets of Marketing Development of Handicrafts in the State of Trpura, *First State Level Marketing Workshop on Handicrafts of Tripura,* 18th August 1998, Agratala, Office of the Development Commissioner (Handicrafts), Ministry of Textiles, Govt. of India, North Eastern Region, Guwahati, 1998.

43. *Development of Bamboo and Cane Sector in India*, Ministry of Environment and Forest, Govt. of India, New Delhi, 1999.

44. *Assam State Gazetteer*, Vol. I, Govt. of Assam, Guwahati, 1999.

45. Dhar, D.N., Artisan of the Paradie, *A Study of Art and Artisans of Kashmir form Ancient to Modern Times*, Bhavan Book and Prints, New Delhi, 1999

46. *Assam, Beyond 2000*, Asom Prakalap, Guwahati, 2000.

47. Saikia, Rajen, *Social and Economic History of Assam*, 1853-1921, Manohar, New Delhi, 2000.

48. Gopalkrishna, R., *Assam Land and People*, Omsons Publications, New Delhi 2000.

49. Liebl, Maureen and Ray, Tirthankar., "Handmade in India: Preliminary Analysis of Crafts Producers and Crafts Productions," *Economic and Political Weekly*, Vol. XXXVIII, Mumbai, 2003.

50. Borah, K.C., Key Note Address in the UGC Sponsored National Level Seminar on *Present Status of Handicrafts in the North-Eastern Region* Held at Gargaon College, Simaluguri, 3rd and 4th February, 2006.

4

A Brief Profile of the Surveyed Districts and Socio-Economic Conditions of the Sample Entrepreneurs

In this chapter an attempt has been made to give a brief profile of the surveyed districts and discuss the socio-economic conditions of the sample entrepreneurs of the cane and bamboo units. Therefore, this chapter is divided into two sections. Section I deals with socio-economic profile of the surveyed districts, while section II incorporates the analysis of the socio-economic conditions of the sample entrepreneurs of the cane and bamboo units.

SECTION - I

A Brief Profile of the Surveyed Districts:

The seven districts of the Brahmaputra valley namely Sivasagar, Tinsukia, Nagaon, Nalbari, Sonitpur, Kamrup and Goalpara were selected for our field study. Brief profile of each district is presented on the basis of the secondary information collected from different sources.

4.1.1. Sivasagar District:

Sivasagar is one of the oldest districts in the state. The district is divided into three Sub-divisions, namely Sivasagar, Charaideo and Nazira Sub-division. Sivasagar district covers an area of 2668 square kilometers as against total area of 78438 square kilometers of Assam. As per 2001 census, out of the total 1051736 population, 954557 persons (90.76%) were living in rural areas and others 97179 persons (9.24%) were living in urban areas of the district. The density of population per square kilometer was 395 as compared to 340 in Assam. There were 926 females for every one thousand males of the district. The literacy rate was 75.33 percent of the district, which is the second higher as compared to 64.28 percent in Assam. The decadal growth rate of population of the district was 15.95 percent which is lower than Assam average (18.85%) during 1991-2001.

A majority of the people of the district derived their livelihood from agriculture and allied activity. About 43.33 percent of workers were engaged in agriculture as compared to 52.36 percent of all Assam as per census 2001. In the field of development of Industry, the district has long history of establishment of first industry. The Assam Company which was established in England in 1839. This was first company to undertake the commercial production of tea in India. The headquarter of the company was situated at Nazira of the district. Nazira remained as the headquarter until this company was shifted to Kolkota in 1965. Tea and coal industry was well established in the district before independence in India. The oil industry is one of the important industry and the eastern regional headquarter of

ONGC (L) is situated at Nazira. The district has 137 registered factories with 6144 average daily workers in 2003-04. Total number of small scale registered industries was 2882 in the district in 2003. As per DICC record there 64 registered cane and bamboo units in the district in 2003. Total gross district domestic product was Rs. 226716 in 2000-01. The per capita gross district domestic product was Rs. 21779 in the district in 2000-01.

4.1.2. Tinsukia District:

Tinsukia is the easternmost district on the southern bank of the state. The district is comprised of Tinsukia, Margherita and Sadiya Sub-division. The district covers an area of 3790 square kilometers and has a population of 1150062 as per the 2001 census. Out of the total population, urban population has been recorded 223957 (19.47%) and rural population as 926105(80.53%) in 2001. The density of population is 303 per square kilometers of the district, which is a little less than state average. There is 909 females for every one thousand males as per the 2001 census. The literacy rate is 63.28 percent as compared to 64.28 percent in Assam. The decadal growth rate of population of the district was 19.52 percent during 1991-2001, which is more against the 18.85 percent of the state.

As per the census of 2001, 37.37 percent of workers were engaged in agriculture which is much lower than all Assam average (5.36%). Since the nineteenth century, Tinsukia had been a centre of trade and industry of the state. Digboi refinery was established in 1901, which is the oldest oil refinery in Asia. Coal mines are located at Lidoo and Margherita and number of plywood factories are established at Makum, Tinsukia and Margherita in the district. A total of 1506 small scale registered industries were accounted in the district in 2003. There were 389 registered factories with 17334 average daily workers in the district in 2003-04. Tinsukia is the district headquarter town, with a busy railway junction. The junction serves as the most important commercial centre of upper Assam. A forest training centre is also located at Makum. The total gross district domestic products was Rs.201507.00 of the district in the year of 2000-01. The per capita gross district domestic product has been estimated at Rs. 17707.00 of the district in 2000-01. The Sadiya town of the district is situated in the remotest corner of Assam.

4.1.3. Nagaon District:

The central district Nagaon is comprised of three sub-division namely Nagaon, Hajoi and Kaliabor. The district headquarter town Nagaon is located at 123 kilometers away from Guwahati. The district covers an area of 3831 square kilometers with a population of 2314629 as per census of 2001. Out of the total population, 2036342 (87.98%) are rural and 278287 (12.02%) are urban population in the district. The density of population per square kilometer in the district was 604 persons in 2001 census, which is must higher than the state. It may be noted here that Nagaon district ranked first, regarding density of population among the all districts of Assam. The sex ratio in terms of females per thousand males was 939 in the district. The literacy rate was 62.28 percent, which is also less as compared to 64.28 percent in Assam. The decadal growth rate of population was 22.30 percent in the district, which is much higher than the state average.

The economy is mainly agrarian and 58.28 percent of workers engaged in agriculture as compared to 52.36 percent of Assam as a whole as per the census of 2001. The district is identified as one of the industrially backward district of Assam. A sugar mill is located at Kampur. There were 3065 registered small scale industries as on 2003 in the district. There were 103 registered factories with 3386 average daily workers in the district. The district covered 2268 kilometer length of roads under P.W.D. in the year 2004. The total gross district domestic product was accounted for Rs. 185054.00 in the year 2000-01. The per capita gross district domestic product was accounted for Rs. 8081.00 in 2000-01. A fishery training collage is situated at Raha in the district.

4.1.4. Nalbari District:

Nalbari district has only one sub-division. The district is bounded by the Bhutan hills and the Brahmaputra river on the north and south respectively. The district is lagging behind in respect of infrastructural facilities for economic development. The district covers an area of 2257 square kilometer and is inhabited by a population of 1148824 as per census report 2001. Out of the total population, 1121338 (97.61%) were rural and 27486 (2.39%) were urban in the district. The density of population is 504. The sex ratio in terms of females per thousand males of the district was 937 in 2001. The literacy rate was 68.08 percent as compared to 64.28 percent for Assam. The decadal growth rate of population was 11.98 percent in the district as compared to 18.85 percent of the state, as a whole, as per the census of 2001.

The economy of the district mainly depends on agriculture. 70.45 percent of workers were engaged in agriculture, which is high against 52.36 percent of the state as per the census of 2001. The district has not developed industrially. A synthetic spinning mill located at Nathkuchi near Tihu is the only medium type industry of the district.

In the district, total 1744 registered small scale industries were established upto 2003. There were 10 registered factories, with 497 average daily workers in the district in the year 2003-04. Total gross district domestic product has been accounted Rs. 92805.00 in 2000-01. The per capita gross domestic product was Rs. 8169.00 in the district in 2000-01. Total length of road was 1153 kilometers under P.W.D. in the district in 2004.

4.1.5. Sonitpur District:

The district is comprised of Tezpur and Biswanath Chariali sub-division. The town Tezpur is a historic place and it is well connected by road, rail and airways with different places of the state. The district is on the threshold of a new era of economic development with the construction of Bhomoraguri bridge over the Brahmputra river. The north bank district of Sonitpur accounts for 1681513 persons as per the census of 2001. Out of the total population, 1505719 (89.54%) are rural and 175794 (10.46%) are urban population in the district. The area of the district is 5324 square kilometers. The density of population per square kilometers was 315 persons and the sex ratio was 942 in 2001. The literacy rate of the district was 60.29 percent. The decadal growth rate of population of the district is lower (17.80%) as compared to 18.85 percent of the state during 1991-2001.

Agriculture is the way of life for majority of the people in the district. A total of 46.69 percent of workers were engaged in agriculture, which is low as compared with 52.36 percent of the state as per census 2001. The district is also backward in respect of industrial development. A co-operative sugar mill is located at Lehugaon in the district. There were 2404 number of various types of small scale registered industries in the district in 2003. There are 235 registered factories in Sonitpur district with 10029 average daily workers during the year 2003-04. Total gross domestic product of the district has been found to be Rs. 138405.00 in 2000-01. The per capita gross district domestic product was Rs. 8223 in the district in 2000-01. The length of the roads under P.W.D was accounted for 2351 kilometers in 2004. It is to be noted that Tezpur town has been fast growing in commercial and industrial importance after the construction of Bhomoraguri bridge over the Brahmaputra of the state.

4.1.6. Kamrup District:

The district is divided into three Sub-Divisions namely Guwahati, Rangia and Chandrapur. The modern city of Guwahati is the headquarter of the district and the state. Guwahati is also the gateway to the North Eastern region. The total geographical area of the district is 4345 square kilometers. The district was inhabited by a population of 2522324 according to 2001 census. The district shelters the largest population among all the districts of Assam. The urban population has been estimated at 908217 (36%) and the remaining 1614107(64%) is found in rural area as per 2001 census. There were 894 females against every one thousand males of the district. The literacy rate was 74.69 in the district, which is much higher than the state average. The density of population is 579. The decadal growth rate of population for the district was 25.75 percent as against 18.85 percent of the state during 1991-2001. The district is fast growing in education, commercial and industrial importance in the state. As per the census of 2001, 33.63 percent workers were engaged in agriculture in the district, which is lower as compared to 52.36 percent of the state. In the industrial field, the total registered small scale industries were 13928 in the district in 2003. There were 623 registered factories with average daily 12068 workers in the district in 2003-04. The highest registered factories at the district level is observed in Kamrup district in the state. Total gross district domestic product was worth Rs. 556181.00 in 2000-01. The per capita gross domestic product of Kamrup district was valued at Rs. 22292.00 in the year 2000-01. The headquarters of N-F.Railway is located at Guwahati. Besides it has Tea Auction centre of the state. The length of roads under P.W.D. was 2290 kilometers in 2004 in the district. In fact the district is on the threshold of a new era of socio-economic development following the construction of Saraighat bridge. After the construction of Saraighat bridge, it serves as the vital road and rail link of the North Eastern states with the other part of the country.

4.1.7. Golapara District:

Golapara district has only a sub-division. The district covers an area of 1824 square kilometers. The district shelters 822035 persons as against the total 26655528 persons of the state as per census 2001. Out of the total population, 755133 persons (91.86%) were in rural area and the remaining 66902 (8.14%) were in urban area of the district. The literacy rate was 58.56 percent, which is lower than the state average. The density of population per square kilometer was 451 person and the sex ratio was 955 in 2001. The density of population in the district is 451. The decadal growth rate of population for the district was 23.07 percent, which is much higher than the state average in 2001.

Agriculture is the mainstay of the district economy and a total of 55.20 percent of workers were engaged in agriculture as per the census in 2001. Goalpara is one of the industrially backward district of the state. During the decades of planning, no major industry was established in the district.

On the whole, 1412 registered small scale industries were located up to 2003. There were only 7 registered factories with 113 average daily workers in the district during the year 2003-04. The total gross domestic product was of the district estimated at Rs. 62140.00 in 2000-01. The per capita gross district demotic product was valued Rs. 7643.00 in the district in 2000-01. The district had a total P.W.D. road length of 794 kilometers in the year of 2004. Goalpara forest division covers 392.03 square kilometers in area of total reserved forest in the state. It is seen that the construction of Naranarayan Setu over the Brahmaputra river began a new era of socio-economic development of the district which connected Pancha Ratna of Goalpara and Jogighapa of Bangaigaon district of Assam. It is to be noted here that the British East India Company carried on trade relations from Golapara with the Ahom Kingdom before the treaty of Yandaboo in 1826.

SECTION - II

In this section an attempt is made to discuss the socio–economic conditions of the entrepreneurs of the cane and bamboo units covered under our sample study. For this study we have taken the following aspect. These are – year of establishment of enterprises, types of ownership, factors motivated to undertake cane and bamboo works, family background, economic background, previous occupation to under take this enterprises, particular to family, education level, structure of the units, infrastructural facilities, nature of products, technology of production, source of finance, marketing channels, role of middlemen and registration.

4.2.1 Year of Establishment:

Although cane and bamboo works are the oldest traditional crafts in Assam, the items have taken as a

Table 4.1
Year of the Establishment of the Sample Cane and Bamboo Units, 2002-03

Area	*Periods*										*Total Units*
	1951-60	*Percent-age*	*1961-70*	*Perce-ntage*	*1971-80*	*Percent-age*	*1981-90*	*Percent-age*	*1991-2001*	*Percent-age*	
Rural	5	5.81	8	9.30	7	8.14	27	31.40	39	45.35	86
Urban	Nil	-	Nil	-	Nil	-	16	35.56	29	64.44	45
Total	5	3.82	8	6.11	7	5.34	43	32.82	68	51.91	131

commercial venture only in recent time. In order to know the trend as well as sustainability of the commercial production of cane and bamboo units in Assam, informations regarding the year of establishment are collected. The details of classification of sample units as per the year of establishment is shown in Table 4.1

It is observed from Table 4.1 that the majority of sample units were established between 1991-2001. Out of total 86 rural units, 45.35 percent of working units were established between 1991-2001, while 64.44 percent units in urban areas were established during this period. It is to be noted that 5 units in rural areas were reported to have been established during 1951-60. In the contrast to the rural units, all the urban unit were established after 1981. It reflects the fact that commercialism emerged in case of cane and bamboo works in urban areas of Assam in recent year.

4.2.2 Types of Ownership:

The distribution of the types of ownership of the sample cane and bamboo units are given in Table 4.2.

It can be seen from the Table 4.2 that proprietorship concern is the most popular form of cane and bamboo units

Table 4.2
Types of Ownership of the Sample Cane and Bamboo

Area	*Type of Ownership*				*Total*
	Proprietorship	*Percentage*	*Partnership*	*Percentage*	*Units*
Rural	84	97.67	2	2.33	86
Urban	45	100.00	Nil	-	45
Total	**129**	**98.47**	**2**	**1.53**	**131**

in Assam. Out of total 131 sample units, 129(98.47%) units are proprietorship concern, and the rest 2(2.33%) units, are partnership concern. The proprietorship and partnership concern of the rural sample is 84(97.67%) and 2 (2.33%) respectively. All urban sample units are operating under proprietorship. It is pertinent to note that in our sample units none has been reported to operate in co-operative system.

4.2.3 Motivating Factors:

Motivating is an important factor to a person to undertake an enterprise. There are different types of motivating factors which influence a person to undertake an enterprise. Cane and bamboo works is not an exception. It is well known that skill and knowledge of a person about the enterprise is considered the primary factors to motivate him or her. In some cases, individuals undertake an enterprise under compulsion situation. In our field survey we have asked six types of questions to the respondents in this regard. These include economic reason, shortage of land, hereditary, encouragement from relatives and friends and increasing demand for the products. The results are given in Table 4.3

Table 4.3 reveals that among all the factors, more than three fourth of the respondents, ranks first the economic reason and ranks last the increasing market demand by the sample units. So far as rural areas are concerned, out of total 86 rural units, about 67.44 percent units reported that economic reason is the basic motivating factor for establishing cane and bamboo works. Shortage of land is also another determining factor for motivating the entrepreneurs. Hereditary factor was ranked in the third. On the other hand it could be seen from the table that except one, all other

Table 4.3

Factors Motivating to Start the Sample Cane and Bamboo Units, 2002-03

Area	*Motivating Factors*					
	Economic reason	*Percentage*	*Shortage of land*	*Percentage*	*Hereditary*	*Percentage*
Rural	58	67.44	14	16.27	9	10.47
Urban	44	97.78	Nil	-	Nil	-
Total	**102**	**77.86**	**14**	**10.69**	**9**	**6.87**

(Contd.)

(Contd. Table 4.3)

Area	Motivating Factors						Total Units
	Encouragement from relative	Percentage	Encouragement from friend	Percentage	For it increasing market demand	Percentage	
Rural	3	3.49	2	2.33	Nil	-	86
Urban	Nil	-	Nil	-	1	2.22	45
Total	**3**	**2.29**	**2**	**1.53**	**1**	**0.76**	**131**

respondents reported that economic reason as the primary motivating factor for establishing cane and bamboo units. Thus, it is clear from the analysis that economic reason was the main factor for starting the cane and bamboo units in our sample areas.

4.2.4. Family Background:

The majority of the people in rural areas of Assam are obtaining their livelihood from agriculture. But due to low land-man ratio there is heavy pressure on agricultural land. Thus, in many agricultural families, adult members are becoming either unemployed or seasonally unemployed. Finding no opportunity for employment, members of such families undertook cane and bamboo works as full time occupation. Thus, most of the entrepreneurs' family rural areas reported agricultural background. In the urban areas most of the people are associated with service and business. It is seen that due to lack of employment opportunity in the government and private sectors, some urban people have taken cane and bamboo works as a means of livelihood in the state. Therefore, majority of the entrepreneurs' reported family background either service or business. The field survey shows that out of the total 131 sample entrepreneurs of the cane and bamboo units, 63.36 percent sample entrepreneurs come from agricultural families, 18.32 percent from service holders' and 16.79 percent business families. The family background of the rural sample shows that 86.05 percent entrepreneurs are reported of having agriculture as their family background. On the other hand, out of the total 45 urban entrepreneurs, 42.22 percent come from service holders' families and 33.33 percent from businessmen's families. The data regarding family background of the sample entrepreneurs are given in Table 4.4.

Table 4.4

Family Background of the Sample Entrepreneurs of the Cane and Bamboo Units, 2002-03

Area	*Category*								*Total Units*
	Agriculture	*Percentage*	*Business*	*Percentage*	*Service holder*	*Percentage*	*Others*	*Percentage*	
Rural	74	86.05	7	8.14	5	5.81	Nil	-	86
Urban	9	20.00	15	33.33	19	42.22	2	4.45	45
Total	**83**	**63.36**	**22**	**16.79**	**24**	**18.32**	**2**	**1.53**	**131**

Table 4.5

Previous Occupation of the Sample Entrepreneurs of the Cane and Bamboo Units, 2002-03

Area	*Category*								*Total*
	Unemployed	*Percentage*	*Agriculture*	*Percentage*	*Business*	*Percentage*	*Working other Organization*	*Percentage*	*Units*
Rural	39	43.35	27	31.40	10	11.63	10	11. 26	86
Urban	16	35.55	NIL	-	18	40.00	11	24.45	45
Total	**55**	**41.98**	**27**	**20.61**	**28**	**21.38**	**21**	**16.03**	**131**

4.2.5. Previous Occupation:

The living pattern of a entrepreneur is very much influenced by the status and nature of occupation. Occupational structure means the distribution of working force in different occupation such as agriculture, industry and other sectors for their livelihood. There are various factor such as availability of resources, expertise, technical knowledge and level of income on which trends of occupation depend. The previous undertaking of cane and bamboo units in our surveyed districts is reported of having some other occupations before entering into this venture. The entrepreneur of the sample cane and bamboo units have their different background such as unemployment, farmer, petty businessman, temporary worker in private organization etc. The previous occupations of the sample entrepreneurs of the cane and bamboo units have been presented in Table 4.5.

The Table 4.5 revels that out of the total 131 sample entrepreneur, about 42 percent were unemployed, prior to entering this occupation. Similarly 40 percent entrepreneurs were engaged in petty business in urban areas where as it was 11.63 percent in rural areas. About 31.40 percent entrepreneurs have their background as cultivators and all belong to areas. About 16.03 percent entrepreneurs were engaged in other organizations, prior to undertaking the present units.

4.2.6 Population:

The size of population is a an important factor to determine the socio-economic development of a society. An analysis of population requires the knowledge of the socio-economic characteristics, such as family size, sex composition, marital status, religion, educational level, age distribution

Table 4.6
Households Population of the Sample Entrepreneurs of the Cane and Bamboo Units, 2002-03

Area	*Category*				*Total*
	Male	*Percentage*	*Female*	*Percentage*	
Rural	241	55.02	197	44.98	438
Urban	120	54.30	101	45.70	221
Total	**361**	**54.78**	**298**	**45.22**	**659**

etc. All these variables operate in every society leading either to reduction or to enhancement of the level of development. The household-population of the sample entrepreneurs of the came and bamboo units are given by sex in Table 4.6

It is seen from Table 4.6 that the total 131 sample cane and bamboo entrepreneurs have a population of 659 of which 66.46 percent are rural and 33.54 percent are urban. Out of total 438 population of rural sample entrepreneur, 55.02 percent are male and 44.98 percent are female. In the context of the rural population, in urban areas 54.30 percent are male and 45.70 percent are female.

4.2.6.1. Family Size:

It is observed that large family size is another factor to a grater extent, which is responsible for low slandered of living, especially in rural areas. It is seen that rural economies have bigger family size, on economic ground. In contrast to rural areas, large family size has started to disintegrate in the urban economy. The largeness of the family size is explained by the fact that people are maintaining the traditional outlook as an attitude. It is an established fact that small family norm is the best and leads to highly welfare and qualitative life of the entrepreneurs.

Table 4.7
Family Size of the Sample Entrepreneurs of the Cane and Bamboo Units, 2002-03

Area	*Family Size*						*Total Units*
	1-3	*Percentage*	*4-6*	*Percentage*	*7-9*	*Percentage*	
Rural	8	9.30	69	80.23	9	10.47	86
Urban	7	15.56	38	84.44	Nil	-	45
Total	**15**	**11.45**	**107**	**81.68**	**9**	**6.87**	**131**

The data regarding family size of the sample entrepreneurs of the cane and bamboo units are presented in Table 4.7.

It is seen from the Table 4.7 that out of total 131 sample entrepreneurs, the highest number, i.e. 107(81.68%) entrepreneurs belong to the family size group of 4-6. About 11.45 percent entrepreneurs belong to the family size group of 1-3. In urban areas there is no households in the size group 7-9. The average family size of the rural and urban areas are 5.09 and 4.91 persons respectively, which is lower above the state average of 6.5. The average family size worked out to be 5.03 for all the sample units together.

4.2.6.2. Sex Composition:

The entrepreneurs both male and female can play an important role in instigating socio-economic change in a area. The entrepreneurship development is lagging behind for the successful development in the state. It is discouraging to note that there is a lack of entrepreneurial motivation in any trade on the part of the female in the state. Active participation of women in cane and bamboo enterprises have always been low as compared to men. The women are not aware of the importance of entrepreneurship though the income level of

Table 4.8
Sex Composition of the Sample Entrepreneurs of the Cane and Bamboo Units, 2002-03

Area	*Category*				*Total Units*
	Male	*Percentage*	*Female*	*Percentage*	
Rural	86	100.00	Nil	-	86
Urban	43	95.56	2	4.44	45
Total	**129**	**98.47**	**2**	**1.53**	**131**

the family can be raised. In our study out of 131 sample units, only 2 women entrepreneurs were found. However, they belonged to urban areas. The sex complication of the sample entrepreneurs of the cane and bamboo units are shown in Table 4.8.

4.2.6.3. Marital Status:

It is found from the survey that out of total 131 sample cane and bamboo entrepreneurs, 117(89.31%) entrepreneurs are married and 14(10.69%) entrepreneurs are unmarried. In the rural area, 75(87.21%) entrepreneurs are married and the rest are unmarried. The married and unmarried urban sample entrepreneurs are 42(93.33%) and 3(6.67%) respectively. The material status of the sample entrepreneurs of the cane and bamboo units are presented in Table 4.9

Table 4.9
Marital Status of the Sample Entrepreneurs of the Cane and Bamboo Units, 2002-03.

Area	*Category*				*Total Units*
	Married	*Percentage*	*Unmarried*	*Percentage*	
Rural	75	87.21	11	12.79	86
Urban	42	93.33	3	6.67	45
Total	**117**	**89.31**	**14**	**10.69**	**131**

Table 4.10
Religious Status of the Sample Entrepreneurs of the Cane and Bamboo Units, 2002-03

Area	*Hindu*	*Percentage*	*Muslim*	*Percentage*	*Others*	*Percentage*	*Total Units*
			Category				
Rural	67	77.91	16	18.60	3	3.49	86
Urban	38	84.44	7	15.56	Nil	-	45
Total	**105**	**80.15**	**23**	**17.56**	**3**	**2.29**	**131**

4.2.6.4. Religion:

Religion is a system of beliefs, practices and attitudes relating to the sacred and uniting its adherents in a community. It is worth mentioning that all religious people are associated with cane and bamboo entrepreneurship in the state. The religious status of the sample entrepreneurs of the cane and bamboo units have been given in Table 4.10.

It has been observed from Table 4.10 that more than 80 percent entrepreneurs are Hindus while 3 entrepreneurs are reported as coming from other religions. About 17.56 percent entrepreneurs are Muslims.

4.2.6.5. Educational Level:

The basic determinant of the socio-economic development is the expansion of education. The expansion of education can contribute much to accelerate the process of entrepreneurship development. The educational attainment level of the cane and bamboo entrepreneurs are not much satisfactory in the state. As a result, it hampers the overall development of cane and bamboo works in Assam. The data regarding the level of education of the sample entrepreneurs of the cane and bamboo units are shown in Table 4.11.

Table 4.11

Level of Education of the Sample Entrepreneurs of the Cane and Bamboo Units, 2002-03

Area	*Category*								*Total Units*
	Below HSLC	*Percentage*	*HSLC*	*Percentage*	*HSSLC*	*Percentage*	*Graduate*	*Percentage*	
Rural	78	90.70	7	8.14	1	1.16	Nil	-	86
Urban	24	53.33	14	31.11	5	11.11	2	4.45	45
Total	**102**	**77.86**	**21**	**16.03**	**6**	**4.58**	**2**	**1.53**	**131**

Table 4.12

Age Distribution of the Sample Entrepreneurs of the Cane and Bamboo Units, 2002-03

Area	*Age Groups*								*Total Units*
	20-30	*Percentage*	*31-45*	*Percentage*	*46-60*	*Percentage*	*61-Above*	*Percentage*	
Rural	10	11.63	32	37.21	41	47.67	3	3.49	86
Urban	5	11.11	26	57.78	14	31.11	Nil	-	45
Total	**15**	**11.45**	**58**	**44.28**	**55**	**41.98**	**3**	**2.29**	**131**

The Table 4.11 reveals that out of the total 131 sample entrepreneurs, 102 (77.68%) are below HSLC level, followed by HSLC 21 (16.03%), HSSLC 6(4.58%) and graduates 2(1.53%). In the rural areas, 78(90.70%) entrepreneurs are below HSLC level and 7 (8.14%) are HSLC level. It is to be noted that only one entrepreneur is found in the HSSLC passed. Similarly, more than 53.33 percent urban entrepreneurs were found below HSLC. Two entrepreneurs were reported to the graduates in urban areas.

4.2.6.6. Age Distribution:

The working force available in an area determines the performance of cane and bamboo enterprises, because it is a labour intensive enterprise. The data regarding age distribution of the sample entrepreneurs are presented in Table 4.12.

The Table 4.12 reveals that the majority (44.27%) of the entrepreneurs are of the age group of 31-45 years. About 3.49 percent entrepreneurs are of the age group above 60 years and above in the rural area. While all urban entrepreneurs were below 61 years.

4.2.7. Units Structure:

Generally the efficiency of any individual units is influenced by its structure and other facilities available to him. The structure of the sample units in rural and urban areas of the state largely depend on the economic resources of the entrepreneurs. The structure of sample units may be classified into three- categories: Katcha, Semi-Pacca and Pacca. The Katcha unit is made of mud, bamboo, cane, reed, wood and thatch or C.I. Sheet. The floor of such units is also katcha. A semi-pacca unit is one which has katcha walls, roof with C.I. Sheet and pacca floor. In case of pacca units,

Table 4.13
Structure of the Sample Cane and Bamboo Units, 2002-03

Area	*Category*						
	Pacca	*Percentage*	*Semi-Pacca*	*Percentage*	*Katcha*	*Percentage*	*Total Units*
Rural	2	2.33	27	31.40	57	66.27	86
Urban	15	33.33	23	51.11	7	15.56	45
Total	**17**	**12.98**	**50**	**38.17**	**64**	**48.85**	**131**

burnt bricks, cement, iron rods etc. are used in the construction. The sample cane and bamboo units structure can be seen from the Table 4.13

It is seen from the Table 4.13 that out of the total 131 sample units, 48.85 percent units structure are katcha and 38.17 percent unit structures are semi-pacca. Only 12.98 percent unit structure are pacca.The majority (66.27%) of unit structures are katcha in rural area. In the urban area the majority (51.11%) of unit structures are semi-pacca.

4.2.8: Electricity and Telephone Facilities:

Electricity facility is one of the most important component of infrastructure for cane and bamboo entrepreneurship development. Similarly, telephone facility is most essential for proper functioning of the enterprises. It is observed that provision of the two important inputs are nearly limited to the cane and bamboo units covered by out study. The data regarding electricity and telephone facilities of the sample cane and bamboo units are presented in Table 4.14

It is quite clear from the Table 4.14 that out of the total 131 sample units, only 17.56 percent of the units have

Table 4.14
Electricity and Telephone Facilities of the Sample Cane and Bamboo Units, 2002-03

Area	*Units having electricity facility*	*Percentage*	*Units having telephone facility*	*Percentage*	*Total Units*
Rural	2	2.33	Nil	-	86
Urban	21	46.67	5	11.11	45
Total	**23**	**17.56**	**5**	**3.82**	**131**

electricity facility. The electricity facility of the rural and urban sample units is 2.33 percent and 46.67 percent respectively. Only 11.11 percent units in urban sample have telephone facilities

4.2.9. Trained Workers:

It is observed that the sample cane and bamboo entrepreneurs are unable to employ trained workers due to their low capacity to pay higher wages. Therefore, they employ untrained workers who have not obtained any skill. The data in respect of trained workers of the sample cane and bamboo units can be seen in Table 4.15. It is deserved in the Table that only 2 units are reported of having train workers.

Table 4.15
Trained Workers of the Sample Cane and Bamboo Units, 2002-03

Area	*Units having trained Workers*	*Percentage*	*Total Units*
Rural	Nil		86
Urban	2	4.44	45
Total	**2**	**1.53**	**131**

Table 4.16

Nature of Products of the Sample Cane and Bamboo Units, 2002-03

			Category			
Area	*Furniture*	*Percentage*	*Furniture and decorative items*	*Percentage*	*Mats*	*Percentage*
Rural	21	24.42	Nil	-	3	3.49
Urban	10	22.22	19	42.22	2	4.45
Total	31	23.67	19	14.50	5	3.82

(Contd.)

(Contd. Table 4.16)

Area	Category						
	Ordinary japi	*Percentage*	*Fulam japi*	*Percentage*	*Almost all the items*	*Percentage*	*Total Units*
Rural	3	3.49	2	2.32	57	66.28	86
Urban	Nil	-	Nil	-	14	31.11	45
Total	3	2.29	2	1.52	71	54.20	131

4.2.10. Nature of Products:

The sample cane and bamboo units are engaged in producing various items of products. However, many units are specialized in producing particular items. On the basis of type of products, the sample units are classified into six categories, such as furniture producing, furniture and decorative items producing, mats producing, ordinary *japi* producing, *fulam japi* producing and common items producing units. The classification on the basis of products line of the sample cane and bamboo units are shown in Table 4.16.

The Table 4.16 reveals that the highest number of sample units are engaged in producing common items. In the rural area, about 66.28 percent units are associated with producing common items. It is seen that the majority (42.22%) of the urban units are associated with the production of furniture and decorative items whereas it is nil in rural areas. In case of *japi* no, urban units have been as reported as producing this item.

4.2.11. Marketing Channels:

Marketing is considered as an integral part of bringing up production for any enterprise. It is a fact that an efficient marketing channel is a precondition for the development of the cane and bamboo enterprises. The market mechanism of a product involves interest to the producer, the consumer and the middlemen. Divers interests lead the producer to seek a high priced market for his products, the consumer a low priced market and the middleman, a margin between the producers' price and the consumer's price. It is to be noted that consumer is at the centre of the marketing function. Marketing of cane and bamboo product is different from that of the marketing of other industrial products, because traditionally these are produced seasonally. The marketing channels of the sample entrepreneurs are classified into four. These are shown in Table 4.17. Some entrepreneurs marketed their products not only in one channel but also in more than one marketing channels. Miscellaneous marketing channel ncludes sale at fair, middleman, local market, at own units and government agency. The sample cane and bamboo entrepreneurs directly sold their products to the consumer in the fair, local market and own sale at the units.

The Table 4.17 reveals that among the marketing channels, channel IV (Miscellaneous) was found to be the most important as it handled the highest (45.80%) amount of products. The channel IV (Miscellaneous) was the most important in the rural area. This channel handled 55.81 percent of the total products in the rural areas. The next important channel was channel II (Sale at unit premises). Average dealing in this channel was found to be 25.19 percent of the total products. Channel III (Middlemen) was associated with 8.40 percent of total products. In comparisons to the rural areas, the urban area appeared to have the most important channel as found in channel II (At own units) handling 73.33 percent of the total products. The local market handled 31.40 percent of products in the rural areas. It is observed that both rural and urban sample units are associated with channel IV (Miscellaneous). But none of the sample units are found exporting the cane and bamboo products outside the country.

4.2.12 Raw Material:

It is a well known fact that availability of raw materials is very necessary for the smooth running of any individual unit. Raw materials like cane, bamboo, nail, varnish, disposed bicycle tyre, *takou* leaf etc. are used for

Table- 4.17

Marketing Channels of the Sample Cane and Bamboo Units, 2002-03

Marketing channels	*Rural* *Units*	*Percentage*	*Urban* *units*	*Percentage*	*Total* *units*	*Percentage*
I. (Local market): Producer → Consumer	27	31.40	Nil	-	27	20.61
II. (At own units): Producer → Consumer	Nil	-	33	73.33	33	25.19
III.(Middlemen): Producer → Middlemen	11	12.79	Nil	-	11	8.40
consumer	48	55.81	12	26.67	60	45.80
IV.(Misc):Producer → Middlemen / → / Govt. Agency → Consumer						
-	**86**	-	**45**	-	**131**	-

Table 4.18

Sources of Borrowing of the Sample Cane and Bamboo Units, 2002-03

Area	*Sources of borrowing*					*Total Borrowing Units*	*Percentage*	*Units having own fund only*	*Percentage*
	Co-operative Society	*Nationalized Bank*	*Trader*	*Money lender*	*Relative*				
Rural	1	Nil	3	2	1	7	8.14	79	91.86
Urban	Nil	4	5	Nil	Nil	9	20.00	36	80.00
Total	**1**	**4**	**8**	**2**	**1**	**16**	**12.21**	**115**	**87.79**

the cane and bamboo works. But, these raw materials are not available locally at all times. It is found that out of the total sample units, 71.76 percent of the units are reported to have faced problems in respect of regular supply of raw materials. The 69.77 percent rural and 75.56 percent urban sample units have faced similar problem in getting of regular supply of raw materials for cane and bamboo works.

4.2.13. Sources of Finance:

Availability of finance is the basis of every enterprises for expansion and modernization of production process. Money is required for short period as well as for long period in order to improve the production process and the marketing network for the cane and bamboo enterprises. Some of the sample entrepreneurs undertaking cane and bamboo works do not have sufficient money in both rural and urban areas. Therefore, the sample entrepreneurs borrow money from different sources. However, it is reported that many sample units face the problems of getting their required amount of credit. The data regarding borrowing from different sources of the sample units are presented in Table 4.18.

The Table 4.18 reveals that out of the total 131 sample units, only 12.21 percent of the units have borrowed money from different sources. The role of traders in supplying loan to the cane and bamboo units is highest in both in rural and urban area. Out of the total 86 rural sample units, 8.14 percent units have taken loan from co-operative society, trader, money lender and relatives. In contrast, 20 percent urban sample units have taken loan from nationalized bank and traders.

4.2.14 Technology of Production:

The technology is defined as the application of tools, equipments and knowledge for producing useful goods for the people. Generally in cane and bamboo works only simple tools and equipment are required. The tools and equipments like *dao, vhana,* blow lamp, knife, scissors, tongs, saws, hammer, pincers etc. are generally used by sample entrepreneurs for the making of cane and bamboo items. It is observed from the field survey that all 131 sample entrepreneurs have been using traditional technique of production. The modern technique of production has not yet become popular to the sample entrepreneurs. Among many reasons the traditional outlook and low income of the entrepreneurs are the main reasons for non adoption of modern technology. It is also true that modern technology is costly which is not reachable to many of the entrepreneurs. Information was collected from the sample entrepreneurs regarding the from the sample units regarding their views on modern technology for cane and bamboo works. The results are given in Table 4.19.

Table 4.19
Units Expressed their Views on Modern Technology, 2002-03

Area	*Category*				*Total*
	Modern technology required	*Percentage*	*Modern technology not required*	*Percentage*	*Units*
Rural	23	26.74	63	73.26	86
Urban	31	68.89	14	31.11	45
Total	**54**	**41.22**	**77**	**58.78**	**131**

It is seen from the Table 4.19 that out of the total sample entrepreneurs, 41.22 percent entrepreneurs opined about importance of modern technology. It is seen that

26.74 percent rural entrepreneurs and 68.89 percent urban entrepreneurs are in favor of modern technology for cane and bamboo works. The traditional techniques of production has remained the general practice for majority of sample units for cane and bamboo works.

4.2.15. Role of Middlemen:

It is an established fact that the existence of middlemen in marketing process is very essential. Because goods produced in remote areas, is difficult to market in any other areas where there is more demanded for the products. In our study, there are some middlemen who have been found to supply different type of raw materials and money-advance to some entrepreneurs for cane and bamboo works. In that process, the middlemen get their scope to exploit the entrepreneurs especially in the rural area by purchasing the products at low price. In our sample, 12.79 percent units sold their products to the middlemen in rural area. The urban sample units are mostly free from exploitation of the middlemen.

4.2.16. Registration:

The cane and bamboo units are normally registered with District Industrial Center and Commerce (DICC) under the government of Assam. The registered units generally get some benefit from the government. In spite of government support, some entrepreneurs have not been interested in registration of their units. The field survey reveals that out of the total 131 sample units, only 26.72 percent units have registered with the DICC. Registered units in rural and urban areas separately, are 20.93 percent and 37.78 percent respectively. As a result, the majority of sample units have been reported of being deprived of government support. The relevant information's are given in Table 4.20

Table- 4.20
Registration of the Sample Cane and Bamboo Units With District Industries Center and Commerce, 2002-03

	Category				
Area	*Registered*	*Percentage*	*Non Registered*	*Percentage*	*Total Units*
Rural	18	20.93	68	79.07	86
Urban	17	37.78	28	62.22	45
Total	**35**	**26.72**	**96**	**73.28**	**131**

5

Economics of Cane and Bamboo Units

In this chapter an attempt is made to analyses the economics of cane and bamboo units of the sample entrepreneurs of the surveyed districts. For this purpose cost and income analysis for cane and bamboo units covered by our survey separately for rural and urban is made. It is to be noted that as the items produced in the units are of various types, item wise estimation of cost and income can not be made. Thus, our effort will be a modest attempt towards this end.

5.1. Cost Analysis:

Cost of production is the most significant factor governing the supply of a product. It may be noted that cost is the money outlay of a firm on the processes of production of its outputs. For the estimation of cost in cane and bamboo works, there are some inherent conceptual and statistical difficulties. According to the National Income Committee in India[1], the available statistics especially small-scale industries are extremely unreliable and incomplete. This view of the committee is more or less applicable in cane and bamboo enterprise also. Most of the cane and bamboo entrepreneurs, whose relevant data were collected, are mostly unfamiliar with the notions and methods of keeping business records. Moreover most of the sample units are operating under family enterprise system. The costs for cane and bamboo works are divided under two broad heads, i.e., variable cost and fixed cost.

5.1.1. Variable Cost:

The variable cost of cane and bamboo units are those costs that do vary with the size of its output. We have divided the variable cost into four heads, i.e., manpower cost, raw materials cost, marketing cost including transportation and other costs. Cost on working capital, telephone, electricity, postal, training of workers and some other contingencies are included in other costs head. Human labourer consists of wages–paid permanent or temporary hired laboures, family laboures and own laboures engaged in cane and bamboo activities. The amount paid to hired labourers are worked out on the basis of the prevailing wages rate for own labour. The labour cost is estimated on the basis of the number of days devoted to cane and bamboo works. The man day is defined as the 8 hours work in a day. The principles of evaluation of the wage rates are given in Annexure- IX. Table 5.1 to show the district wise distribution of variable cost for cane and bamboo units covered by our survey.

It reveals from the Table 5.1 that manpower cost occupied the highest (57.80%) among variable costs of the rural sample units. However compare to rural sample a little higher (58.73%) manpower cost is found in urban units. Another important item of variable cost is raw materials, which has been estimated at 24.83 percent of the total cost

Table 5.1

Distribution of Variable Cost Per Unit of Cane and Bamboo Units in Different Districts, 2002-03 (In Rs.)

Sl. No	*Districts*	*Number of Total Rural Units*	*Number of Total Urban Units*	*Variable Cost of Various Heads*			
				Manpower		*Raw Materials*	
				Rural Units	*Urban Units*	*Rural Units*	*Urban Units*
1	Sivasagar	17	9	13575.41 (61.08)	17622.11 (58.11)	4897.29 (20.09)	6092.67 (20.09)
2	Tinsukia	13	4	13717.77 (60. 08)	19824.75 (58.85)	5345.46 (23.41)	8480.00 (25.17)
3	Nagaon	10	7	10490.10 (52.48)	22657.00 (62.99)	5543.70 (27.73)	6485.86 (18.03)
4	Nalbari	13	4	12103.92 (56.29)	13216.50 (47.43)	5536.00 (25.75)	8670.00 (31.12)
5	Sonitpur	15	5	11189.40 (55.70)	18503.20 (58.05)	5111.73 (25.44)	7578.00 (23.77)
6	Kamrup	11	6	14304. 65 (59.76)	19824.83 (58.67)	5757.73 (24.05)	7530.00 (22.29)
7	Goalpara	7	10	10490.00 (55.48)	18503.30 (60.23)	5646.71 (29.86)	6003.00 (19.54)
Total	-	86	45	12441.71 (57.80)	18796.91 (58.73)	5345.21 (24.83)	6931.89 (21.66)

(Contd.)

(Contd. Table 5.1)

Marketing		*Others*		*Total*	
Rural Units	*Urban Units*	*Rural Units*	*Urban Units*	*Rural Units*	*Urban Units*
2284.18 (10.28)	3809.56 (12.56)	1467.24 (6.60)	2800.42 (9.24)	22224.12	30324.76
2424.62 (10.62)	3540.00 (10.51)	1345.47 (5.89)	1845.23 (5.47)	22833.32	33689.98
2533.80 (12.68)	4261.57 (11.85)	1422.16 (7.11)	2564.97 (7.13)	19989.76	35969.40
2530.92 (11.77)	3646.00 (13.09)	1330.62 (6.19)	2330.15 (8.36)	21501.46	27862.65
2431.20 (12.10)	3664.00 (11.50)	1357.74 (6.76)	2130.11 (6.68)	20090.07	31875.31
2573.36 (10.75)	4133.33 (12.23)	1302.10 (5.44)	2302.14 (6.81)	23937.84	33790.31
1613.57 (8.53)	3656.00 (11.90)	1158.45 (6.13)	2558.01 (8.33)	18908.73	30720.31
2379.78 (11.06)	3834.24 (11.98)	1357.58 (6.31)	2442.30 (7.63)	21524.28	32005.34

(Figures within parenthesis indicate percentage of row total)

for rural units. Whereas, it is 21.66 percent for urban units. Almost equal amount of marketing cost is evident for rural and urban sample units. Out of the total variable cost 6.31 percent cost is found for others variable items cost; for rural units and 7.63 percent for urban units. The average annual per unit variable cost is the highest (Rs. 23937.84) in the Kamrup district and the lowest (Rs. 18908.73) is Goalpara district of the rural sample units. On the other hand, the average annual per unit variable cost is the highest (Rs. 35969.40) in the Nagaon district and lowest (Rs. 27862.65) is found in the Nalbari district of the urban sample units. It is observed that the average annual per unit variable cost of the urban areas is higher in compare to the rural areas

5.1.2. Fixed Cost:

The fixed costs of cane and bamboo units are those costs that do not vary with the size of its output. This includes the costs of fixed plant and equipment used in units. The furniture and instruments, rent on building and other costs are included in fixed cost for cane and bamboo works. The depreciation cost and interest on fixed capital are included in other costs of the sample units. This fixed cost has to be borne by the cane and bamboo units even when it is temporarily shut down and thus produce nothing. The finding of the fixed cost of rural and urban sample units have been summarized in Table 5.2 separately for rural and urban units.

Table 5.2 reveals that more than eighty percent (82.87%) of the total cost incurred for rent on building in rural areas. In the urban areas, total 78.86 percent cost is estimated for rent on building, which is lower in comparison to rural units. The principle of evaluation of the rent rates are given in Annexure-IX. The furniture and instruments

Table 5.2

Distribution of Fixed Cost Per Unit of Cane and Bamboo Units in Different Districts, 2002-03 (In Rs.)

Sl. No	Districts	Number of Total Rural Units	Number of Total Urban Units	Fixed Cost of Various Heads: Furnisher and Instruments		Rent on Building (Rental + Own)		Others		Total	
				Rural Units	Urban Units	Rural Units	Urban Units	Rural Units	Urban Units	Rural Units	Urban Units
1	Sivasagar	17	9	1258.05 (14.87)	3357.89 (18.80)	6888.35 (81.41)	13667.92 (76.50)	314.51 (3.72)	839.48 (4.70)	8460.91	17865.29
2	Tinsukia	13	4	1161.00 (13.66)	3161.25 (17.58)	7050.54 (82.93)	14034.63 (78.03)	290.25 (3.41)	790.31 (4.39)	8501.79	17986.19
3	Nagaon	10	7	1042.10 (12.78)	3099.14 (16.91)	6848.45 (84.02)	14454.54 (78.86)	260.53 (3.20)	774.79 (4.23)	8151.08	18328.47
4	Nalbari	13	4	1085.07 (12.85)	3085.00 (17.04)	7091.02 (83.94)	14252.93 (78.71)	271.26 (3.21)	771.25 (4.25)	8447.35	18109.18
5	Sonitpur	15	5	1112.00	3212.40	9612.89	13993.00	278.00	803.10	8302.89	18008.50

(Contd.)

(Contd. Table 5.2)

Sl. No	Districts	Number of Total Rural Units	Number of Total Urban Units	Fixed Cost of Various Heads: Furnisher and Instruments		Rent on Building (Rental + Own)		Others		Total	
				Rural Units	Urban Units	Rural Units	Urban Units	Rural Units	Urban Units	Rural Units	Urban Units
6	Kamrup	11	6	(13.39)	(17.84)	(83.26)	(77.70)	(3.35)	(4.46)		
				1369.02	3469.17	7561..21	14569.46	342.25	867.29	9272.48	18905.87
7	Goalpara	7	10	(14.76)	(18.35)	(81.55)	(77.06)	(3.69)	(4.59)		
				1060.14	2060.00	7053.36	13192.42	265.04	515.00	8378.54	15767.42
				(12.65)	(13.06)	(84.19)	(83.67)	(3.16)	(3.27)		
Total	-	86	45	1164.73	2986.16	7042.64	13925.5	291.1[illegible]	746.5	8498.5[illegible]	17658.23
				(13.71)	(16.91)	(82.87)	(78.86)	(3.42[illegible]	(4.23		

(Figures within parenthesis indicate percentage of row total)

for rural units have accounted for 13.71 percent, which is also lower in comparison to 16.91 percent of urban units. Among other fixed costs, depreciation is one of the important item in the cost of production of the commodity. There is some depreciation of fixed assets in producing items. Every year a cane and bamboo entrepreneur has to bear this loss on account of depreciation. The rate of depreciation cost applied in computing the values of all tools and machines are shown in Annexure-IX. Depreciation cost and interest on fixed capital are included in other heads of costs, because those costs are very nominal for cane and bamboo works. About 4.23 percent cost is occupied in other fixed cost heads in urban units, where as it is 3.42 percent in the rural units. The average annual per unit fixed cost of the rural units is between Rs. 8151.08 to Rs. 9272.48 and in the urban units it is between Rs. 15767.42 to Rs. 18905.87 for the districts covered by our study. It is observed that the average per unit fixed cost of the urban units is higher in comparison to rural units.

5.1.3. Total Production Cost:

The total annual production cost of the sample cane and bamboo units is estimated by adding the total annual variable production cost and total annual fixed production cost for cane and bamboo works. The data regarding total cost of production of the sample units separately for rural and urban units are presented in Table 5.3 Table 5.4 shows percentage distribution of aggregate of different items of cane and bamboo production of the sample units.

The Table 5.3 reveals that out of average annual production cost 71.69 percent is found as variable cost and 28.31 percent is estimated as fixed cost for rural sample units. In contrast, about 64.44 percent is found as variable cost

Table 5.3
Distribution of Total Cost Per Unit of Cane and Bamboo Units in Different Districts, 2002-03 (In Rs.)

Sl. No	*Districts*	*Number of Total Rural Units*	*Number of Total Urban Units*	*Variable Cost*		*Fixed Cost*		*Total Cost*	
				Rural Units	*Urban Units*	*Rural Units*	*Urban Units*	*Rural Units*	*Urban Units*
1	Sivasagar	17	9	22224.12 (72.43)	303224.76 (62.93)	8460.91 (27.57)	17865.29 (37.07)	30685.03	48190.05
2	Tinsukia	13	4	22833.32 (72.87)	33689.98 (65.19)	8501.79 (27.13)	17986.19 (34.81)	31335.11	51676.17
3	Nagaon	10	7	19989.76 (71.03)	35969.40 (66.24)	8151.08 (28.97)	18328.47 (33.76)	28140.84	54297.87
4	Nalbari	13	4	21501.46 (71.79)	27862.65 (60.61)	8447.35 (28.21)	18109.18 (39.39)	29948.81	45971.83
5	Sonitpur	15	5	20090.07 (70.76)	31875.31 (63.90)	8302.89 (29.24)	18008.50 (36.10)	28392.96	49883.81)
6	Kamrup	11	6	23937.84 (72.08)	33790.31 (64.12)	9272.48 (27.92)	18905.87 (35.88)	33210.32	52696.18
7	Goalpara	7	10	18908.73 (69. 30)	30720.31 (66.08)	8378.54 (30.70)	15767.42 (33.92)	27287.27	46487.73
Total	-	**86**	**45**	**21524.28 (71.69)**	**32005.34 (64.44)**	**8498.55 (28.31)**	**17658.24 (35.56)**	**30022.83**	**49663.58**

(Figures within parenthesis indicate percentage of row total)

Table 5.4
Distribution of Share of the Different Cost of Production of Per Unit in Different Districts, 2002-03 (In Percentage)

Item of variable cost	*Sivasagar*		*Tinsukia*		*Nagaon*	
	Rural Units	*Urban Units*	*Rural Units*	*Urban Units*	*Rural Units*	*Urban Units*
Manpower	44.24	36.57	43.78	38.36	37.28	41.73
Raw materials	15.96	12.64	17.06	16.41	19.70	11.94
Marketing	7.44	7.91	7.74	6.85	9.00	7.85
Others	4.78	5.81	4.29	3.57	5.05	4.72
Sub Total	72.43	62.93	72.87	65.19	71.03	66.24
Item of fixed cost	-	-	-	-	-	-
Furnisher and instruments	4.10	6.97	3.71	6.12	3.70	5.71
Rent on building	22.45	28.36	22.50	27.16	24.34	26.61
Others	1.02	1.74	0.93	1.53	0.92	1.43
Sub Total	27.57	37.07	27.13	34.81	28.97	33.76
Total Production cost	**100.00**	**100.00**	**100.00**	**100.00**	**100.00**	**100.00**

(Contd.)

(Contd. Table 5.4)

Nalbari		Sonitpur		Kamrup		Goalpara	
Rural Units	*Urban Units*	*Rural Units*	*Urban Units*	*Rural Units*	*Urban Units*	*Rural Units*	*Urban Units*
40.42	28.75	39.41	37.09	43.07	37.62	38.44	39.80
18.48	18.86	18.00	15.19	17.34	14.29	20.69	12.91
8.45	7.93	8.56	7.35	7.75	7.84	5.91	7.87
4.44	5.07	4.78	4.27	3.92	4.37	4.25	5.50
71.79	60.61	70.76	63.90	72.08	64.12	69.30	66.08
-	-	-	-	-	-	-	-
3.62	6.71	3.92	6.44	4.12	6.58	3.89	4.43
23.68	31.00	24.35	28.06	22.77	27.65	25.85	28.38
0.91	1.68	0.98	1.61	1.03	1.65	0.97	1.11
28.21	39.39	29.24	36.10	27.92	35.88	30.70	33.92
100.00	**100.00**	**100.00**	**100.00**	**100.00**	**100.00**	**100.00**	**100.00**

and the remaining 35.56 percent is fixed cost for urban sample units. The variable cost is found to be the highest (72.87%) in Tinsukia district in the rural units, where in urban units it is found to be the highest (66.24%) in the Nagaon district. The variable cost is lowest (69.30%) in Goalpara district in the rural areas, where it is 60.61 percent in Nalbari district in urban units. In case of fixed cost, Goalpara district is accounted to be the highest (30.70%) and Tinsukia district is the lowest (27.13%) in the rural units. The fixed cost is estimated to be the highest (39.39%) in Nalbari district and Nagaon district is found to be the lowest (33.76%) in the urban units. The average annual per unit cost of production in rural areas is found to be the highest (Rs. 33210.32) in Kamrup district, where it is estimated to be the highest (Rs. 54297.87) in Nagaon district in urban areas. The average annual per unit cost of production is lowest (Rs. 27287.27) in Goalpara district in the rural areas and in the urban area it is lowest (Rs.45971.83) in the Nalbari district for cane and bamboo works. The percentage distribution of the different items of cost as shown in Table 5.4 revealed that manpower is found highest among other cost. The rent (house rent) was found second highest. As expected, marketing cost in rural areas is found higher than the urban counterpart.

5. 2 Production Analysis:

The supply of goods and services come out of production. The value of production refers to the value of the total items produced in a given time period. It is to be noted that the estimation of the income of the sample cane and bamboo units is subject to various conceptual and practical difficulties. The most of the sample entrepreneurs are still currying on production at a family level or are running household enterprise on a small scale. Some of the sample entrepreneurs have no idea of maintaining accounts and do not feel it necessary to maintain regular accounts as well. They also do not disclose their income easily and correctly. Under such a situation it is really a difficult task to collect the adequate data. In this respect, the National Income Committee of India[2] mentioned that an element of guess-work, therefore, invariably enters into the assessment of output, especially in the large sector of the economy which are dominated by the small producer or the household enterprise. However, effort are being made in the field survey to solve these difficulties so as to find out correct estimates of production, sale and income of the sample entrepreneurs. In this analysis, the total production and sale, total income, net income, income per unit separately for rural and urban cane and bamboo units are included.

5.2.1 Production and Sale:

The production of cane and bamboo items were influenced by its selling pattern. On the other hand, selling pattern of cane and bamboo items is determined by the entrepreneurs' financial strength. Items produced in cane and bamboo units in our study, have already been discussed (Chapter IV in Table 4.16). The information of production and sale of the rural and urban sample units are shown in Tables 5.5 and 5.6.

It is seen from the Table 5.5 that as high as 97.03 percent of the produce of the rural units have been sold and the remaining 2.97 percent is kept as inventory. Among the districts under study, the highest (97.35%) amount of products is sold in Nagoan district and the lowest amount (96.09%) amount is sold in Nalbari district. In contrast to rural units, about 96.75 percent products is sold and rest 3.25 percent is kept as inventory in urban areas (Table 5.6).

Table 5.5
Per unit Total Production and Sale of the Cane and Bamboo Units in Different Districts, 2002-03 (In Rs.) (Rural)

Sl. No	*Districts*	*Number of Total Rural Units*	*Sale*		*Inventory*		*Production*	
			Total Sale	*Sale*	*Total Inventory*	*Inventory*	*Total Production*	*Per Unit Production*
1	Sivasagar	17	583270.00 (97.30)	34310.00	16156.00 (2.70)	950.35	599426.00	35260.35
2	Tinsukia	13	451311.00 (96.77)	34716.23	15083.00 (3.23)	1160.23	466394.00	35876.46
3	Nagaon	10	319500.00 (97.35)	31950.00	8685.00 (2.65)	868.50	328185.00	32818.50
4	Nalbari	13	436012.00 (96.09)	33539.38	17758.00 (3.91)	1366.00	453770.00	34905.38
5	Sonitpur	15	463130.00 (97.34)	30875.33	12664.00 (2.66)	844.27	475794.00	31719.60
6	Kamrup	11	409188.00 (97.19)	37198.91	11827.00 (2.81)	1075.18	421015.00	38274.09
7	Goalpara	7	208016.00 (97.29)	29716.57	5795.00 (2.71)	827.86	213811.00	30544.43
Total	-	**86**	**2870427.00 (97.03)**	**33377.06**	**87968.00 (2.97)**	**1022.88**	**2958395.00**	**34399.94**

(Figures within parenthesis indicate percentage of row total)

Table 5.6

Per unit Total Production and Sale of the Cane and Bamboo Units in Different Districts, 2002-03 (In Rs.) (Urban)

Sl. No	Districts	Number of Total Urban Units	Sale		Inventory		Production	
			Total Sale	Sale	Total Inventory	Inventory	Total Production	Per Unit Production
1	Sivasagar	9	466922.00 (97.04)	51880.22	14250.00 (2.96)	1583.33	481172.00	53436.55
2	Tinsukia	4	220659.00 (97.28)	55164.75	6164.00 (2.72)	1541.00	226823.00	56705.75
3	Nagaon	7	407225.00 (97.16)	58175.00	11885.00 (2.84)	1697.86	419110.00	59872.86
4	Nalbari	4	197999.00 (95.61)	49499.75	9095.00 (4.39)	2273.75	207094.00	51773.50
5	Sonitpur	5	267010.00 (96.76)	53402.00	8930.00 (3.24)	1786.00	275940.00	55188.00
6	Kamrup	6	341386.00 (96.16)	56897.67	13628.00 (3.84)	2271.33	355014.00	59169.00
7	Goalpara	10	493768.00 (96.76)	49376.80	16523.00 (3.24)	1652.30	510291.00	51029.10
Total	-	**45**	**2394969.00 (96.75)**	**53221.53**	**80475.00 (3.25)**	**1788.33**	**2475444.00**	**55009.87**

(Figures within parenthesis indicate percentage of row total)

Tinsukia district reveals the highest (97.28%) sale, where Nalbari district shows the lowest (95.61%). Kamrup district was found the highest for the per unit production in both rural (Rs. 38274.09) as well as urban (Rs. 59169.00) units. The average annual per unit production reveals lowest in Goalpara district for both rural (Rs. 30544.43) and urban (Rs. 51029.10) units. It is observed that less inventory is left in rural units. It is because of that low capacity to holding the products for future favorable price.

5.2.2. Gross Income, Net Income and Income Per Unit:

In our analysis income was taken as the value of production of the units. The gross income represents the value of total sale of production and the inventories of the units. The net income per unit is found out by deducting total production cost of cane and bamboo works from gross annual income of the sample units. The average total annual income per unit is found out by adding net income and average family labour cost per unit plus rental value of the own establishment. It is to be noted that for calculation of total income of an unit the rental value of the owned building is also included, because while calculating the cost of production this amount is added.

Tables 5.7 and 5.8 represent the district wise gross income, net income, annual average income per unit and income per family workers separately for rural and urban areas. It is seen that from cane and bamboo the average annual net income as well as average total income per unit (including family income and rental value of building) both rural and urban areas are found the highest in Kamrup district. So, far as average family workers engaged in cane and bamboo units is concerned, less number is found in urban units than the rural units. It is because of the fact that urban

Table 5.7

Per unit Gross Income, Net Income and Income of the Cane and Bamboo Units in Different Districts, 2002-03 (In Rs.)(Rural)

Sl. No	*Districts*	*Number of Total Rural Units*	*Gross Income*	*Production Cost*	*Family Labour Cost*	*Rental Value (Own Building)*
1	Sivasagar	17	35260.35	30685.03	9600.12	6888.35
2	Tinsukia	13	35876.46	31335.11	9760.08	7050.54
3	Nagaon	10	32818.50	28140.84	6785.00	6848.45
4	Nalbari	13	34905.38	29948.81	9280.08	7091.02
5	Sonitpur	15	31719.60	28392.96	9920.00	6912.89
6	Kamrup	11	38274.09	33210.32	9792.09	7561.21
7	Goalpara	7	30544.43	27287.27	10080.29	7053.36
Total	-	**86**	**34399.91**	**30022.83**	**9368.01**	**7042.64**

(Contd.)

(Contd. Table 5.7)

Net Income	*Total Income Per Unit*	*Average Number of Family Workers*	*Average Income to Family Workers Per Unit*
4575.32	21063.79	2.12	4528.36
4541.35	21351.97	4.08	2392.18
4677.66	18311.11	2.10	3230.95
4956.57	21327.67	3.08	3013.01
3326.64	20159.53	3.13	3169.33
5063.77	22417.07	2.36	4149.19
3257.16	20390.81	3.14	3210.28
4377.08	**20787.23**	**4.84**	**3432.70**

(Figures within parenthesis indicate percentage of row total)

Table 5.8

Per unit Gross Income, Net Income and Income of the Cane and Bamboo Units in Different Districts, 2002-03 (In Rs.)(Urban)

Sl. No	*Districts*	*Number of Total Urban Units*	*Gross Income*	*Production Cost*	*Family Labour Cost*	*Rental Value (Own Building)*
1	Sivasagar	9	53463.55	48190.05	13760.11	12676.90
2	Tinsukia	4	56705.75	51676.17	13846.25	15025.65
3	Nagaon	7	59872.86	54297.87	12900.14	15354.51
4	Nalbari	4	51773.50	45971.83	12685.00	14352.96
5	Sonitpur	5	55188.00	49883.81	13330.40	14514.22
6	Kamrup	6	59169.00	52696.18	13545.00	15090.63
7	Goalpara	10	51029.10	46487.73	12900.30	13290.24
Total	-	**45**	**55009.87**	**49663.58**	**13270.93**	**13941.87**

(Contd.)

(Contd. Table 5.8)

Net Income	Total Income Per Unit	Average Number of Family Workers	Average Income to Family Workers Per Unit
5273.50	31710.51	1.56	8820.58
5029.58	33901.48	2.25	6153.89
5574.99	33829.64	2.00	6450.07
5801.67	32839.63	3.25	3903.08
5304.19	33148.81	2.20	6059.27
6472.82	35108.45	1.67	8110.78
4541.37	30731.31	2.80	4607.25
5346.29	**32559.09**	**2.20**	**6439.94**

(Figures within parenthesis indicate percentage of row total)

Table 5.9

Per unit Income Comparison of the Rural and Urban Cane and Bamboo Units from Cane and Bamboo Works in Different Districts, 2002-03 (In Rs.)

Sl. No	*Districts*	*Number of Total Rural Units*	*Income from Cane and Bamboo works*	*Number Urban Units*	*Income from Cane and Bamboo Works*	*Income Difference of the Rural and Urban Units*
1	Sivasagar	17	21063.79	9	31710.51	10646.72
2	Tinsukia	13	21351.97	4	33901.48	12549.51
3	Nagaon	10	18311.11	7	33829.64	15518.53
4	Nalbari	13	21327.67	4	32839.63	11511.96
5	Sonitpur	15	20159.53	5	33148.81	12989.28
6	Kamrup	11	22417.07	6	35108.45	12691.38
7	Goalpara	7	20390.81	10	30731.91	10341.10
Total	-	**86**	**20787.73**	**45**	**32559.09**	**11771.36**

(Figures within parenthesis indicate percentage of row total)

units are more organized and operated under commercial line. District wise variation is also observed. For example average family workers employed in the cane and bamboo units is more than four number in Tinsukia district where as it is two number in Nagaon district in the rural areas. Normally it reflects the fact that in rural areas higher number of association of family workers in subsidiary occupation (in this case cane and bamboo works) means higher number of disguised unemployment in agriculture. However, to verified such statement further study is required. The average annual income to family workers working in the craft units for rural and urban areas is Rs. 3432.70 and Rs. 6439.94 respectively for all the districts taken together. Thus, we observe that inter-district inequalities are there in respect of average annual income per unit from cane and bamboo works of the sample districts. A summery finding of the rural and urban income comparison from cane and bamboo works is shown in Table 5.9. It is observed that urban units shown higher income in comparison to rural units. The All India Rural Household Survey[3] shows that the level of income in urban areas is just twice that of the rural areas in our country. Table 5.9 reveals that the level of income of the sample entrepreneurs in rural areas is higher but not twice that of the sample entrepreneurs in rural areas. The rural and urban disparity of income indicates the lack of progress of the cane and bamboo works in rural areas in comparison to urban areas in Assam.

5.2.3 Income From Other Sources:

In addition to cane and bamboo works all the rural units have earned income from agriculture and allied activities. Similarly about 80 percent of urban units have earned income from different types of petty business. The information regarding net income (Gross income minus cost

Table 5.10

Per unit Net Income from Other Sources of the Cane and Bamboo Units in Different Districts, 2002-03 (In Rs.)

(Rural)

Sl. No	*Districts*	*Number of Total Rural Units*	*Units Having Others Income*	*Income from Other Sources*	
				No	*Agriculture*
1	Sivasagar	17	17	14	210753.00 (91.49)
2	Tinsukia	13	13	13	136072.00 (100.00)
3	Nagaon	10	10	7	93820.00 (83.72)
4	Nalbari	13	13	13	139222.00 (100.00)
5	Sonitpur	15	15	11	173870.00 (90.73)
6	Kamrup	11	11	11	144816.00 (100.00)
7	Goalpara	7	7	6	58791.00 (91.59)
Total	-	**86**	**86**	**75**	**957344.00 (94.01)**

(Contd.)

(Contd. Table 5.10)

No	*Income from Other Sources*				
No	*Livestock*	*No*	*Poultry*	*Total Net Income*	*Per Unit Net Income*
1	6348.00 (2.76)	2	13250.00 (5.75)	230351.00	13550.06
-	-	-	-	136072.00	10467.08
-	-	3	18246.00 (16.28)	112066.00	11206.60
-	-	-	-	139222.00	10709.38
4	17775.00 (9.27)	-	-	191645.00	12776.33
-	-	-	-	144816.00	13165.09
-	-	1	5400.00 (8.41)	64191.00	9170.14
5	**24123.00 (2.37)**	**6**	**36896.00 (3.62)**	**1018363.00**	**11841.40**

(Figures within parenthesis indicate percentage of row total)

Table 5.11

Per unit Net Income from Other Sources of the Cane and Bamboo Units in Different Districts, 2002-03 (In Rs.) (Urban)

Sl. No	*Districts*	*Number of Total Urban Units*	*Units Having Other Income*	*Income from other Sources Business*	*Per Unit Net Income*
1	Sivasagar	9	6	85213.00	14202.17
2	Tinsukia	4	4	53786.00	13446.50
3	Nagaon	7	5	55102.00	11020.04
4	Nalbari	4	4	41185.00	10296.25
5	Sonitpur	5	5	85113.00	17022.60
6	Kamrup	6	5	95011.00	19002.20
7	Goalpara	10	7	69196.00	9885.14
Total	-	**45**	**36** (80.00)	**484606.00**	**13461.28**

(Figures within parenthesis indicate percentage)5.2.4. Total Family Income:

of production) from other sources of the sample units are presented in Tables 5.10 and 5.11.

Table 5.10 reveals that as expected agriculture occupied highest (94.01%) sources of other income of the cane and bamboo units in our study in rural areas. In addition to agriculture, households earned supplementary income from livestock and poultry. But the shares of their sources are small. The average annual per unit net income from other sources of the rural units is between Rs. 9170.14 to Rs. 13550.06. The average annual per unit income from other sources is highest (Rs. 13550.06) in Sivasagar district and the lowest (Rs. 9170.14) in Goalpara district. It is seen from the Table 5.11 that in case of urban units the average annual per unit net income from other sources is highest (Rs. 19002.20) in Kamrup district and the lowest (Rs. 9885.14) in Goalpara district. It is observed that there exists inter-district inequalities in receipts of income from other sources in both rural and urban units.

5.2.4. Total Family Income :

The total family income from cane and bamboo works and other sources of the sample units are presented in Tables 5.12 and 5.13 separately for rural and urban areas. We have also made an attempt to estimate the per capita income of the family members of the surveyed cane and bamboo units in order to have a comparison with that of state average and the variability among the districts. For this purpose, state average per capita income of Rs. 12074.00 (Assam Economic Survey 2002-2003) figure is compared with our findings.

The Table 5.12 reveals that in the rural areas, average 63.71 percent of total income has been estimated from cane and bamboo works and the remaining 36.29 percent worked out to be from other sources. The average annual per unit total income from all sources of rural units is the highest (Rs

Table 5.12

Per Unit Total Income from Cane and Bamboo Works and Other Sources of Income in the Cane and Bamboo Units in Different District, 2002-03 (In Rs.) (Rural)

Sl.No	*Districts*	*Number of Total Rural Units*	*Income from Cane and Bamboo Works*	*Income Income from Other Sources*	*Total Income from all Sources*	*Average Family Size*	*Per Capita Income*
1	Sivasagar	17	21063.79 (60.85)	13550.06 (39.15)	34613.85	5.06	6840.68
2	Tinsukia	13	21351.97 (67.10)	10467.08 (32.90)	31819.05	5.46	5827.66
3	Nagaon	10	18311.11 (62.03)	11206.60 (37.97)	29517.71	5.40	5466.24
4	Nalbari	13	21327.67 (66.57)	10709.38 (33.43)	32037.05	4.69	6830.93

(Contd.)

(Contd. Table 5.12)

Sl.No	Districts	Number of Total Rural Units	Income from Cane and Bamboo Works	Income Income from Other Sources	Total Income from all Sources	Average Family Size	Per Capita Income
5	Sonitpur	15	20159.53 (61.21)	12776.33 (38.79)	32935.86	4.40	7485.42
6	Kamrup	11	22417.07 (63.00)	13165.09 (37.00)	35582.16	4.70	7570.67
7	Goalpara	7	20390.81 (68.98)	9170.14 (31.02)	29560.95	6.86	4309.18
Total	-	**86**	**20787.73 (63.71)**	**11841.43 (36.29)**	**32629.16**	**5.09**	**6410.45**

(Figures within parenthesis indicate percentage of row total)

Table 5. 13

Per Unit Total Income from Cane and Bamboo Works and Other Sources of Income in the Cane and Bamboo Units in Different Districts, 2002-03 (In Rs.) (Urban)

Sl.No	*Districts*	*Number of Total Urban Units*	*Income from Cane and Bamboo works*	*Income Income from Other Sources*	*Total Income all Sources*	*Average Family Size*	*Per Capita Income*
1	Sivasagar	9	31710.51 (69.07)	14202.17 (30.93)	45912.68	4.33	10603.39
2	Tinsukia	4	33901.48 (71.60)	13446.50 (28.40)	47347.98	5.25	9018.67
3	Nagaon	7	33829.64 (75.43)	11020.04 (24.57)	44849.68	4.43	10124.08
4	Nalbari	4	32839.63 (76.13)	10296.25 (25.87)	43135.88	5.50	7842.89

(Contd.)

(Contd. Table 5.13)

Sl.No	*Districts*	*Number of Total Urban Units*	*Income from Cane and Bamboo works*	*Income* *Income from Other Sources*	*Total Income all Sources*	*Average Family Size*	*Per Capita Income*
5	Sonitpur	5	33148.81 (66.07)	17022.60 (33.93)	50171.41	4.00	12542.85
6	Kamrup	6	35108.45 (64.88)	19002.20 (35.12)	54110.65	5.00	10822.13
7	Goalpara	10	30731.91 (75.66)	9885.14 (24.34)	40617.05	5.80	7002.94
Total	-	**45**	**32559.09 (70.75)**	**13461.28 (29.25)**	**46020.37**	**4.91**	**9372.78**

(Figures within parenthesis indicate percentage of row total)

35582.16) in Kamrup district and the lowest (Rs.29517.71) in the Nagaon district. It is observed that in rural areas the cane and bamboo works are pursued by the sample entrepreneurs in their spare time as a subsidiary occupation, as their primary occupation is agriculture and allied activities.

So far as highest and lowest total average income of different districts is concerned, a similar picture is observed for urban areas. It is seen that per capita income is the highest (Rs. 7570.67) in Kamrup district where it is lowest (Rs. 4309.18) in Goalpara district in the rural units. The per capita income for Sonitpur, Sivasagar, Nalbari, Tinsukia and Nagaon district is found to be Rs. 7485.42, Rs 6840.68, Rs. 6830.93, Rs 5824.66 and Rs 5466.24 respectively in the rural units. In contrast, the per capita income of the urban units is the highest (Rs. 12542.85) in Sonitpur district and it is found to be the lowest (Rs. 7002.94) in Goalpara district. The per capita income of the urban units in the remaining districts viz, Kamrup, Sivasagar, Nagaon, Tinsukia and Nalbari district Rs. 10822.13, Rs 10603.39, Rs. 10124.08, Rs 9018.67 and Rs 7842.89 respectively. It is observed that the per capita income of the households population of the both rural and urban units of the surveyed districts except urban units of Sonitpur district is low in comparison to per capita income of Assam (Rs. 12074.00) in the year 2002-03. It is to be noted that the per capita income of our estimates includes the rental value of own building used for cane and bamboo units. Infact, it reflects the fact that the cane and bamboo units in Assam is not in a position to provide remunerative income to the families in rural and urban areas. Thus, our hypothesis that cane and bamboo works are not remunerative to the entrepreneurs in Assam is accepted.

5.2.5. Break-Even Analysis:

In other to find out profitability from the cane and bamboo works, break-even point (BEP) (in terms of sale) of the sample units under study was worked out. In the estimate of break-even point (in terms of sale) the rural and urban sample units, the sample units are segmented into two- (I) rural (II) urban.

The study of cost-volume profit analysis is often known as break-even analysis. It involves the study of relationship between costs, volume and profit at different levels of sales or production. The break-even point can be defined as that point of sales volume at which total revenue is equal to total cost. The break-even pint is a point of no profit; no loss. A business may be said to be break-even when its total sales are equal to its costs. The break-even is referred to that level of output which evenly break the cost and revenues. It is to be noted that if the production or sales is increased beyond this level, there shall be profit to the firm and if it is decrease from this level, there shall be less to the firm. In our study a modest attempt is made to apply the concept of the profit/ volume ratio to find out the break-even point (in terms of sale) separately for average representative units in both in respect rural areas and urban areas. The results are as follows.

5.2.5.1. Rural Units:

The P/V ratio establishing the relationship between contributions of sales is very significant for analyzing the profitability of operations of a business. The equation of the P/V ratio is expressed as under:

$$\text{P/V Ratio} = \frac{\text{S-V}}{\text{V}} \times 100$$

As we know that the total variable cost of an average representative firm/unit, total fixed cost of average representative firm/unit and total sale of average representative firm/unit of the rural cane and bamboo business firm is Rs 21524.28, Rs 8498.55 and Rs. 33377.06 respectively. Hence, the P/V ratio of the rural business firm can be found as:

$$\text{P/V Ratio} = \frac{33377.06 - 21524.28}{33377.06} \times 100$$

$$= \frac{11852.78}{33377.06} \times 100$$

$$= \frac{11852.78}{33377.06}$$

$$= 35.51\%$$

Using the above data P/V ratio, we calculate the break-even point (BEP) (in terms of sale) as under.

BEP (in terms of sale) of the rural business firm:

$$\text{BEP} = \frac{\text{Fixed Cost}}{\text{P/V Ratio}}$$

$$= \text{Rs. } \frac{8498.55}{35.51\%}$$

$$= \text{Rs. } \frac{8498.55}{35.51} \times 100$$

$$= \text{Rs. } \frac{849855.00}{35.51}$$

$$= \text{Rs. } 23932.84$$

The excess of budgeted sales over the break-even sales is generally known as the margin of safety. The size of the margin of safety is an essential indicator of the strength of a business firm. The larger margin of safety represents that the business is sound and even if there is a substantial decline in sales, there will be some profit of the business firm. The small margin of safety represents that strength of the business is comparatively weak and even a small fall in the sales would adversely impact the profit of the business and may result into losses. The margin of safety of the rural units can also be calculated. The margin of safety may be expressed as below:

Margin of Safety = Total Sales - Sales at Break-Even point. The margin of safety for the rural business firm can be found as:

Margin of Safety = Rs. 33377.06 – Rs. 23932.84 = Rs. 9444.22

5.2.5.2. Urban Units:

In respect of urban cane and bamboo business firm, we know that the total variable cost of an average representative firm/unit, total fixed cost of average representative firm/unit and total sale of average representative firm/unit is Rs.32005.34, Rs 17658.32 and Rs 53221.53 respectively. Hence, the P/V ratio of the urban business firm can be found as:

$$\text{P/V Ratio} = \frac{\text{S-V}}{\text{V}} \times 100$$

$$\text{P/V Ratio} = \frac{53221.53 - 32005.34}{53221.53} \times 100$$

$$= \frac{21216.19}{53221.53} \times 100$$

$$= \frac{2121619.00}{53221.53}$$

$$= 39.86\ \%$$

Using the data above P/V ratio, we calculate the break-even point (BEP) (in terms of sale) as under.

BEP (in terms of sale) of the urban business firm:

$$BEP = \frac{\text{Fixed Cost}}{\text{P/V Ratio}}$$

$$= \text{Rs. } \frac{17658.23}{39.86\ \%}$$

$$= \text{Rs. } \frac{17658.23}{39.86} \times 100$$

$$= \text{Rs. } \frac{1765823.00}{39.86}$$

$$= \text{Rs. } 44300.63$$

The calculating of margin of safety of the urban business firm can be found as follows:

Margin of Safety = Total Sales - Sales at Break-Even point. The margin of safety for the rural industry can be found as:

Margin of Safety = Rs. 53221.53 - Rs. 44300.63 = Rs 8920.90

References

1. Quoted by Chapra, P.N., in *Business Economics*, Kalyani Publisher, New Delhi, 1988, p. 491.

2. Quoted by Dutta, Ruddar and Sundharam, K.P.P., in *Indian Economy*, S Chand and Company Ltd., New Delhi, 1991, p. 40.

3. Quoted by Dhar, P.K., in *Indian Economy, Its Growing Dimensions*, Kalyani Publishers, New Delhi, 2004, p. 72.

6

Problems and Prospects of Cane and Bamboo Works in Assam

The basic objective of our study is to examine the economics of cane and bamboo units, which is fulfilled by the analysis of the preceding chapter (Chapter-V). As our ultimate aim is to ascertain the problems and to assess the prospects of cane and bamboo works in Assam, we try to examine here the problems comforting the cane and bamboo works which have emerged from the analysis of the preceding chapter, and the prospects that have been postulated, based on the observation and analysis. For the analytical purpose, this chapter is divide into two sections. Section I deals with the problems associated with the cane and bamboo works while the Section II incorporates the prospects of cane and bamboo works in the state.

SECTION - I

The development of cane and bamboo works in Assam are remained under developed due to various problems.

Though the severity of a particular problem may vary from unit to unit, there are certain problems which are common to all types of cane and bamboo units. The cane and bamboo artisans being faced various problems for marketing of the products in both rural and urban areas of Assam. Each of the problems of cane and bamboo works have varying significance and not of equal magnitude and importance for the artisans. It is to be noted here that not only cane and bamboo crafts but also other crafts faced with innumerable problems in the state. Of these the lacks of proper infrastructural facilities are major problems on the part of handicrafts development including cane and bamboo works in the state. The limited raw materials source, unorganized production base, limited market opportunities, lack of modernization efforts, lack of proper guidance and encouragement, limited credit facilities, high production cost, stiff competition from the quality products from other states and lack of exposures are the major problems faced by the handicrafts in Assam. In this respect, Assam Handicrafts Survey conducted in 1982 revealed that the peculiar topographical features, shortage of raw materials, low production capacity, finance, competition with the other products and lack of new designs are the major problems which have been collectively and severally hampering the growth of the handicrafts including cane and bamboo in Assam.[1] It is to be noted that the entire North Eastern region is also facing some major problems in the growth of traditional cane and bamboo works. As far as the cane and bamboo crafts is concerned, it can be stated that the crafts are still in the traditional stage in the state and fails to compete with the stiff competition of cheap machine made products. Although, there is a huge potential for the development of cane and bamboo crafts in Assam, but the state has remained backward in the development of this crafts. In the time of field investigation, the cane and bamboo entrepreneurs were asked to rank ten important problems that they are facing for running the units through questionnaire (Appendix III). It is being felt that these major problems are not only hindering the development of cane and bamboo works in the surveyed districts, but also effected the growth of cane and bamboo works in Assam in general. Table 6.1 gives information regarding the identification of the problems faced by the entrepreneurs as per their ranking in rural and urban areas of the surveyed districts.

Table- 6.1
Problems Ranked by Respondents of the SurveyedCane and Bamboo Units, 2002-03

Sl.No	*Problems*	*Rural Ranks*	*Urban Ranks*
1.	Lack of Finance	52(60.46)	28(62.22)
2	Stiff Competition with other products	8(9.30)	7(15.56)
3	High cost of production	5(5.81)	-
4	Marketing Problem.	5(5.81)	3(6.67)
5	Non availability of raw materials	4(4.65)	3(6.67)
6	Lack of systematic guidance	3(3.49)	2(4.44)
7	Limited transport and communication facilities	3(3.49)	-
8	Lack of proper training facilities	2(2.33)	-
9	Design of the products	2(2.33)	2(4.44)
10	Excessive market levy	2(2.33)	-
Total	-	**86(100.00)**	**45(100.00)**

(Figures within parenthesis indicate percentage)

It is seen from the table that in rural areas total problems reported is ten where as in urban areas entrepreneurs reported six problems stand in the way of development of cane and bamboo crafts,

6.1.1. Lack of Finance:

Lack of finance is one of the major problems for organizing successfully the cane and bamboo works in Assam. It could be seen from Table 6.1 that among the all the problems, lack of finance the respondents rank first for both rural and urban units. Finance is required by the artisans to meet their business obligations. Various types of credit is needed by the artisans. The short term loans are required for meeting the current expenditure on articles like purchase of various types of raw materials, and payment of wages etc. On the other hand, medium-term loans are needed for purchase of fixed assets like construction of work shed, machinery and other equipments. Most of the artisans, particularly in rural areas are poor and they are to depend on money lenders and traders to meet their financial needs. Generally the credit facilities are not available from commercial banks and other financial institutions to the artisans. As they are poor and do not have land to mortgage for security and are deprived of the loan facility available from the financial institutions. It has been reported that whatever credit facility is available, it is not easy to obtain from the bank. The tedious process involved in getting a loan, lack of information about financial scheme and harassment by officials for delaying the process showing one plan to other are some of the major problems experienced by the respondents. In the absence of adequate financial arrangements the entrepreneurs fail to expand the cane and bamboo work to desired level. It revealed from the field survey that out of the total 131 surveyed units only 16 (12.21 %) units (Chapter-IV in Table 4.18) have availed financial assistance either from banks or other sources.

Table 6.2

Reasons for not Availing Credit from Institutional Agencies, 2002-03

Sl. No	*Reasons*	*Rural Units*	*Urban Units*	*Total Units*
1	Procedural Complexity	47(54.65)	27(60.00)	74(56.49)
2	Timely not available	17 (19.77)	11(24.45)	28(21.37)
3	Unable to insist any security	12(13.95)	-	12(9.16)
4	Not aware of institutional credit	7(8.14)	-	7(5.34)
5	Inadequate amount of credit	-	2(4.44)	2(1.53)
6	Harassment of official personnel	3(3.49)	5(11.11)	8(6.11)
Total	-	**86(100.00)**	**45(100.00)**	**131(100.00)**

(Figures within parenthesis indicate percentage)

Information was collected from the respondents regarding the reasons for not availing credit from financial institutions and the results are presented in Table 6.2.

It is seen from the Table 6.2 that out of the total 131 sample entrepreneurs, about 56.49 percent entrepreneurs (54.65 in the rural areas and 60 percent in the urban areas) have not taken credit from institutional agencies due to procedural complexity. About 19.77 percent rural sample entrepreneurs reported of not availing credit been use of timely not available, this reason is stated by 24.45 percent urban entrepreneurs. Harassment of officials is also another factor for which the sample entrepreneurs have expressed their anguiness for not availing credit from institutional agency. About 3.49 percent rural and 6.11 urban sample entrepreneurs have experienced harassment of officials. It is also observed that government departments and financial institutions have not yet formulated easy financial scheme for the cane and bamboo artisans. It is strongly felt that such type of easy accessibility of credit from the financial institutions will help in development of cane and bamboo crafts in the state. To have an idea about the credit position of the artisans of the village industries in Assam from commercial banks, we present information published by the govt. of Assam in Table 6.3.

We find from Table 6.3 that outstanding Rs. 1987.37 cores of the total credit available only 2.57 percent were availed by the artisans and village industries as on march, 1996. Out of the total outstanding credit of Rs. 2994.02 cores as on march, 2000, the share of artisans and village industries came down to 1.76 percent. One can conclude from the observation that the commercial banks have also failed to provide necessary finance to the handicrafts sector in the state.

Table 6.3
Distribution of Outstanding Credit of Scheduled Commercial Banks to Artisans and Village Industries in Assam During 1996-2000, (In Rs.)

Sl. No	*Sector*	*March 1996*	*March 2000*
1.	Artisans and village industries	51.01 (2.57)	52.80 (1.76)
2.	Other sectors	1936.36 (97.43	2941.22 (98.24)
Total	**Total bank credit**	**1987.37 (100.00)**	**2994.02 (100.00)**

(Figures within parenthesis indicate percentage)

6.1.2. Stiff Competition with other Products:

The cane and bamboo products of the state is facing increasing competition from the organized industrial products particularly plastic, steel and aluminum. Besides, the cane and bamboo articles produced in the state have to face the competition with the similar imported products and with superior quality within the country. It is also an undeniable fact that in the national market, the quality and design of Assam products, especially handicrafts made of cane and bamboo is compared as not to the mark. The competition between machine made articles and the handicrafts was started during the British period. It is a hard fact that the growth of the factory system of mass production was the cause for the increasing competition between machine made products and handicrafts products during the later part of the British rule. The emergence of rich classes in the British period preferred articles of the factory goods to native handicrafts products including cane and bamboo for social and political reason in Assam. It can be stated that the economic reforms increased competition between cane and bamboo products and cheap industrial products. Due to the competition with other products like plastic, steel and aluminum, cane and bamboo artisans sometime go for distress sale of their products to the traders and middlemen. About 9.30 percent rural and 15.56 percent urban entrepreneurs reported (Table 6.1) that stiff competition with other products is one of the problems for growth and development of cane and bamboo works.

6.1.3. High Cost of Production:

It is the basic problem for 5.81 percent rural sample entrepreneurs (Table 6.1) for cane and bamboo works. The cane and bamboo industry products are facing an increasing trend in its cost of production due to increase of price of the raw materials. Besides, high costs of transport, communication and labour, adds to the higher price of cane and bamboo articles. The selling price of cane and bamboo products was mainly dependent on quality and on total demand and supply in the market. It is observed that competition from cane and bamboo products brought into state from other parts also cause a great harm to the stability and growth of cane and bamboo industry in Assam. For some artisans it is difficult to pay considerably high prices to raw material and other inputs. The knowledgeable entrepreneurs reported that quality raw material; better training and use of labour saving tools will greatly increase the output and will reduce cost of production in the cane and bamboo works.

6.1.4. Marketing Problem:

Efficient marketing system can stimulate production and can increase income of the artisans. It is a fact that the market and marketing forces that determines products,

Figure 6.1
Characteristics of Cane and Bamboo Products Creating Problems in Marketing.

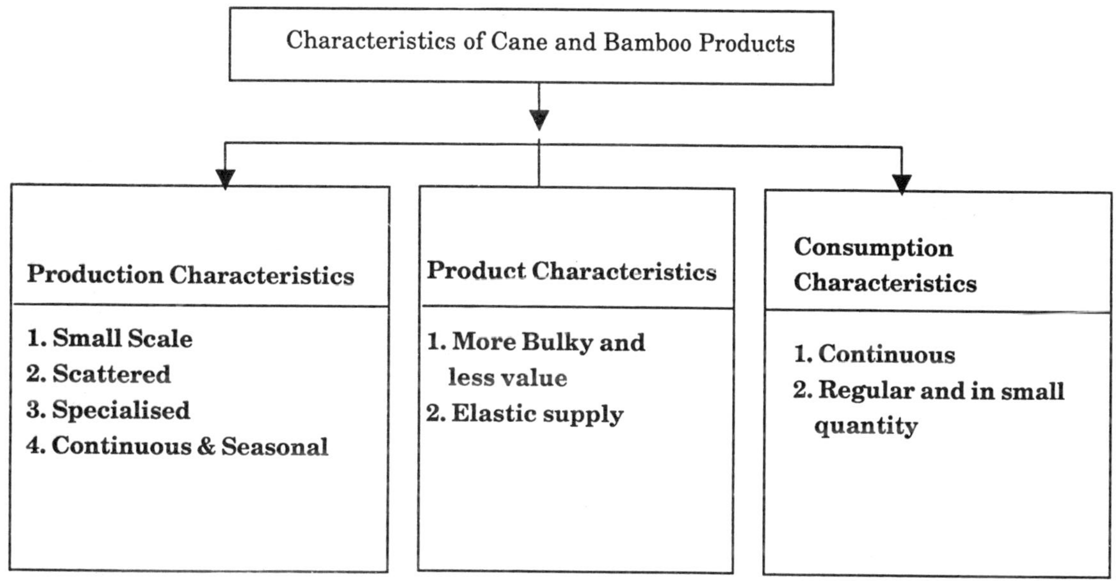

distribution and profit of a product. Hence, marketing has emerged as the centerpiece of entrepreneurial activities. It has been generally realized that lack of proper marketing facility stands on the way of expansion and modernization of cane and bamboo works in the state. The artisans who produce even quality products, cannot profitably sell at a remunerative price due to lack of proper marketing system. Besides the inadequate infrastructural facilities there are certain characteristics of cane and bamboo products which create problems in marketing process as depicted in figure 6.1.

In Table 6.1 it is seen that marketing Problem is the basic problems for 5.81 percent rural and 6.67 percent urban entrepreneurs for development of cane and bamboo works. As a result few products of cane and bamboo works Assam could sell in the national and international market. The cane and bamboo units do not have proper marketing network to sell their products. The rural artisans sell their articles at low margin of profits as they lack of bargaining power. In fact, artisans get into a vicious circle, inadequate marketing facility results low prices for their products and wastage of time, which further leads to low production and again low prices of the products. We have asked the respondents' view regarding the basic problem of marketing of their produce, summary of which is shown in Table 6.4

Table 6.4 reveals that out of the total sample entrepreneurs, the highest (42.75%) entrepreneurs reported that stiff competition with other products is the main problem of marketing the products. About 38.37 percent rural entrepreneurs reported that the stiff competition with other products is the main problem, where

Table 6.4
Marketing Problems Faced by the Entrepreneurs, 2002-03

Sl. No	*Problems*	*Rural Units*	*Urban Units*	*Total Units*
1	Stiff competition with other products	33 (38.37)	23 (51.11)	56 (42.75)
2	Lack of transport and communication facilities	21 (24.42)	11 (24.44)	32 (24.43)
3	Non availability government agency	16 (18.60)	7 (15.56)	23 (17.56)
4	Market too far from the production centre	9 (10.47)	3 (6.67)	12 (9.16)
5	Failed to introduce new design	7 (8.14)	1 (2.22)	8 (6.10)
Total	-	**86 (100.00)**	**45 (100.00)**	**131 (100.00)**

(Figures within parenthesis indicate percentage)

as 51.11 percent of the urban entrepreneurs reported that stiff competition is the basic cause of marketing of cane and bamboo articles. Lack of transport and communication facilities is the second highest problem of marketing ranked by about one fourth of the sample entrepreneurs bought for rural and urban areas. Generally the cane and bamboo artisans have to dispose of their items in local markets. In local market, traders and middlemen from outside, get the scope to exploit the artisans. If such a situation arises in the market then they have to sell the cane and bamboo items at very low prices. The craftsmen of Assam usually produce cane and bamboo items to meet the demand of their local consumers. However, with the introduction of modern design, cane and bamboo products are marketed outside the state. It is clear from the forgoing analysis that the cane and bamboo units are facing a number of problems in the way of their marketing functions due to lack of proper infrastructural facilities in both rural and urban areas. Table 6.4 reveals that the entrepreneurs are facing five major problems in marketing their products. These problems have arisen due to inadequate and insufficient infrastructural facilities in the state. The lack of infrastructural problems in marketing faced by many artisans are no longer able to achieve significant gain from cane and bamboo works. Thus, one of the hypothesis chosen for our study that, there is no proper infrastructural facilities for development of cane and bamboo works in Assam is accepted.

6.1.5. Non Availability of Raw Materials:

Non availability of raw materials is another basic problem for the development of cane and bamboo craft 4.65 percent rural and 6.67 percent urban entrepreneurs (Table 6.1) ranked this problem in the fifth Advisory Committee on Industry constituted by the government of Assam noted that availability of raw materials is the main problem for the artisans in Assam.[2] In respect of raw materials it may be mentioned that despite the species diversity of cane and bamboo available in Assam only a handful species are suitable for this handcrafts. The local name of cane and bamboo species used as raw materials in handicrafts industry in Assam is shown in Table 6.5

It can be seen from Table 6.5 that thirteen number of species of bamboo and eleven number of species of cane are used by the artisans of Assam. The raw materials, particularly bamboo is locally available in the state. But cane is not available in the all locations where this craft is operated. In these areas cane is collected from Nagaland, Arunachal Pradesh and Maghalaya. Generally the raw materials are collected from homesteads, local market and

Table 6.5
Local Name of Cane and Bamboo Species Used as Raw Materials in Handicrafts Industry. 2002-03

Sl. No	*Local name of bamboo*	*Local name of cane*
1	Bhaluka	Lejai
2	Bijuli	Jatibet
3	Mukal	Houka
4	Jati	Chulibet
5	Kakoa	Raiding
6	Lota	Jeng
7	Madang	Sundibet
8	Boro	Hatibet
9	Dalu banh	Panibet
10	Muli banh	Wane
11	Worra	Sialhauka
12	Betibanh	-
13	Nangal banh	-
Total	**13**	**11**

Source: Field Study.

natural forests. The gap between the demand and supply of cane and bamboo as a raw material is increasing day by day for the last few years due to deforestation in the state. The raw materials of cane are mostly purchased by artisans from unauthorized traders who generally operate without any valid forest permit of the state. The traders control the price of cane in the market. Moreover, there is also seasonal fluctuation of the price of raw materials. Considering the non-availability of raw materials, Advisory Committee on Industry has suggested that social forestry department should go for cane and bamboo plantation so that the artisans can find their raw material locally at a reasonable price.[3]

6.1.6. Lack of Systematic Guidance:

Lack of systematic guidance for design, market demand for cane and bamboo works are considered significant problem for this craft. About 3.49 percent rural and 4.44 percent urban entrepreneurs (Table 6.1) ranked this problem in the sixth. At present there is no private initiative in this direction. Thus, the progress cane and bamboo handicrafts in Assam. But, it is generally seen that the officials are not sincere and dedicated. There fore, the implementation of the various programmes and schemes are mostly made half-heartedly in Assam. The organizations like NEHHDC, AGMC, ARTFED, DIC, KVIB, KVIC and CBTC functions are not at all encouraging for all artisans in the state. For achieving a level of development of cane and bamboo sector in a smooth manner, it is very essential to maintain an efficient and clean administration on the part of these organizations. It is discouraging to note that red-tapism in the administration is causing unnecessary delay in the implementation of the programme for the artisans. The most of the cases the artisans are not aware of the

Table 6.6
Proportion of Entrepreneurs Reported Awareness of Government Scheme Regarding Cane and Bamboo Works, 2002-03.

Sl.No	*Awareness of Government Scheme*	*Rural Units*	*Urban Units*	*Total Units*
1	Fully aware	11 (12.79)	14 (31.11)	25 (19.08)
2	Partially aware	32 (37.21)	31 (68.89)	63 (48.09)
3	Not aware	43 (50.00)	- 	43 (32.83
Total	-	**86** **(100.00)**	**45** **(100.00)**	**131** **(100.00)**

(Figure within parenthesis indicate percentage)

government schemes. Information was collected from the sample entrepreneurs regarding their a awareness of development scheme on cane and bamboo works, summary of which is presented in Table 6.6

Table 6.6 reveals that only 19.08 percent of respondents are reported fully aware of the government scheme whereas as 48.09 percent of the sample entrepreneurs are partially aware the schemes. About fifty percent of the rural sample entrepreneurs are not aware of government scheme only 12.79 percent of the rural sample entrepreneurs are fully aware.

The artisans do not have necessary information and guidance about the price, transport and communication in different markets. It is also necessary to provide systematic guidance and encouragement to the concerned organization and agency for the cane and bamboo artisans so that they may wait for better price and profit of their products. The personnel of Handicrafts Corporations of both centre and state did not make a concerted effort to solve the problems being faced by the cane and bamboo artisans in the field of production, finance and marketing in the state. Workshop and seminar is very essential for artisans to bring awareness about the use of new tools, methods and equipments in the production of more value added items. But, very few workshops and seminars so far are organized in the cane and bamboo artisans in Assam.

6.1.7. Lack of Proper Transport and Communication Facilities:

A well developed transport and communication facilities is another important condition for rapid development of handicrafts industry in Assam. It has been observed that handicrafts including cane and bamboo works face the problem of poor transport and communication facilities specially in the rural areas of Assam. Lack of proper transport and communication facilities is the basic problem for 3.49 percent rural sample entrepreneurs (Table 6.1). Cheap and easy means of transport and communication encourage the artisans to carry their produce to markets and create confidence among the artisans and improve their bargaining power. No doubt, a little development has been made in respect of both railway and road communication but only a small number of artisans are linked by railways and pucca roads. The means of transport of carrying the cane and bamboo items are: by-cycle, rickshaw and thala in the rural areas. It is a well known fact that this transport method is labour wastage and time consuming process. Hence, cane and bamboo artisans are kept away from getting reasonable return for his products in the market. In the urban areas, the rich artisans generally use trucks, jeeps, lorries and delivery vans to carry their products to the market. The cane and bamboo industry cannot develop unless villages and towns are made accessible through modern communication like roads, railways, waterways and airways facilities to reduce the transport cost in production and marketing in Assam. It is discouraging to note that the quality of railway network is very poor in the state as compared to that of the country. The total railway routes under broad gauge, in the state, is about 18.96 percent as compared to the 60.6 percent of the country as a whole in 1993-94. The telecommunication facilities have also not been growing slowly in rural Assam, as compared to the national average. Though telephone services are available in all urban areas, this service is not available in all rural areas in Assam. It is observed that due to lack of transport and communication facilities, it is difficult on the part of rural cane and bamboo artisans to sell their products outside markets. Therefore, the artisans have to dispose of their cane and bamboo items in daily and weekly markets, where traders and middlemen from outside get the scope of exploiting the artisans.

6.1.8. Lack of Proper Training Facilities:

Training is required not for making one a good artisan only but also to help in making him a good citizen. It helps in building favorable attitudes towards the profession of the artisans. In Assam, the cane and bamboo works were learnt traditionally in families. Due to lack of proper training facilities the cane and bamboo artisans are still following traditional methods and produce articles of outdated design and styles. With low quality and old design products, the cane and bamboo artisans cannot stand in the competition with the other states. In this connection, it is to be noted that for providing better training facilities and up gradation of skill of the handicrafts artisans, the government of India has set up many training institutes in the country. For instance, the Development Commissioner for Handicrafts, Indian Institute of Entrepreneurship and Cane and Bamboo Technology Centre at Guwahati had so far organized few training programmes for cane and bamboo artisans in the State. But problem is that the craft trainers do not have scope to update their training regularly. Besides, there is no incentives in the form of scholarship, free boarding and lodging for training of the cane and bamboo artisans. Moreover, it has been observed that the small cane and bamboo items producers are unable to employ trained artisans as they do not have capacity to pay higher wages. Generally they employ those labourers who are illiterate and have no trained knowledge by paying low wage. They use outdated methods of production which results in low quality of their items. Therefore, the result is that small artisans fail to compete with the big producers. About 2.33 percent rural sample entrepreneurs reported that lack of proper training facilities as the basic problem of development of cane and bamboo works (Table 6.1). Therefore Handicrafts Organizations and NGOs should make effort to impart training, particularly to rural artisans.

6.1.9. Design of the Products:

Design is considered as an important component for cane and bamboo products. Up to date design of the products is the basic problem with 2.33 percent rural sample entrepreneurs (Table 6.1). A good and attractive design plays its own role in selling of cane and bamboo products, which are purchased by the rich class as decorative pieces. It may be mentioned that new design of cane and bamboo crafts can create demand for its products. In Assam, it is observed that at present the cane and bamboo industry is being run with traditional design. The Handicrafts Organizations and the concerned NGOs have given little attention for the design development and techniques of cane and bamboo works in Assam. The innovation and research on development new design of cane and bamboo crafts are absent in particularly the rural areas of Assam. This is also one of the reasons why the cane and bamboo products do not find a good market in the state. The artisans in Assam have generally failed to create new design of cane and bamboo items according to tastes and preferences of the consumers. The artisans have failed to adopt new methods of production and thus used to be produce old and outdated traditional design of products.

6.1.10. Excessive Market Levy:

In the rural areas the market charges are very high in the local markets. The high market charges are affecting the incentives to work, saving and investment of the artisans. The local excessive market levy has put the cane and bamboo units in a disadvantageous position in rural areas. The local tax structure is not proposition to the price received by the artisan of cane and bamboo works. The poor cane and bamboo artisans are paying a higher market levy, which further leads to higher prices in selling of their items. The high rate market levy have been creating problem for not only cane and bamboo works but also reducing the investible surplus of the cane and bamboo industry. To encourage the investment in the cane and bamboo works the present tax structure should be modified in favour of poor cane and bamboo artisans. It is reported by the artisans that the local tax system stand in the way of cane and bamboo works. It is seen from Table 6.1 that excessive market levy is the basic problem for 2.33 percent of rural sample entrepreneurs.

SECTION - II

From the previous analysis it is observed that the cane and bamboo works are experiencing numerous of problems problem for which this crafts remained unsuccessful enterprise in Assam. In the context of economic liberalization the question arises what will be the future role of cane and bamboo works in strengthening the economy of Assam. Under the existing situation another question also arises whether the cane and bamboo units will be able to survive in Assam. To answer these questions we have to examine the prospects of this enterprise in Assam. Knowledgeable person and officials of the industry reported that the cane and bamboo works has good prospects for development through diversification of products and modernization process. It is encouraging to note that some cane and bamboo items of this state could be able to attract the large number of visitors and tourists at many market places, emporia, exhibitions, fairs etc. In this section attempt is made to examine the prospects of development of cane and bamboo enterprise in respect of employment generating, income generating, foreign exchange earning, sustainable development and entrepreneurship development in the state.

6.2.1. Employment Opportunity:

The unemployment problem is one of the major problems in Assam. It is a hard fact that the additional employment generated in each successive plan period could not keep pace with the growing number of unemployed persons in the state. There is no doubt that the established cane and bamboo units will provide employment opportunities to large number of people of the state as these cane and bamboo units are limited capital investment and labour intensive in nature. The cane and bamboo works can positively participate in an effective programme of full employment in both urban and rural areas. It is a fact that there is not yet a wide recognition of the employment potentialities of cane and bamboo works. The cane and bamboo works are particularly very relevant in the context to solve the seasonal, disguised and industrial unemployment problems particularly in rural areas in the state. The establishment of cane and bamboo units will provide employment opportunity to the surplus agricultural labourers as this requires limited capital and solve seasonal unemployment. These units can be started in both rural and urban areas without much problems by the mobilization of factors of production. We can cite good statistics about employment opportunity created by cane and bamboo works in the economy of Assam. It is to be noted that a total of 30 registered cane and bamboo units were found in Sivasagar district in 2000. In these units total 133 persons got employment opportunity, in the district[4]. In Jorhat district, 76 persons were found employed in the 16 registered cane and bamboo units in 1999[5]. According to Lakhimpur District Gazetteers, cane and bamboo industry provided employment to 1133 persons in the district, among them 973 were males and 160 females according to the census 1961.[6] In this respect it may be noted that in a Status Report of Indian Artisans prepared on the basis of census report of 1981 by SRUTI, a Delhi based NGO, the total number of cane and bamboo workers has been estimated at about 8.2 lakhs in the country. This figure has been derived from the census report of 1981[7]. The cane and bamboo works provide full-time occupation to these highly skilled craftsmen who produce high demand products on commercial scale in the rural and urban areas. From these analysis we can say that there is a good prospects of employment to lakhs of people in the cane and bamboo works in the state.

6.2.2. Income Generating:

Unlike other crafts the cane and bamboo craft is a castles and classless craft in the state. In two way income is generated by this crafts. Those who are involved in producing crafts are getting income out of the sales of the products. Some others accrue their income by supplying raw materials. It is equally important that cane and bamboo can be grown on marginal and waste lands in a short period of time. Thus, growing cane and bamboo can be alternative economic pursuit for the small formers. The cane and bamboo items have good regeneration and are income oriented, which indicate their suitability in developing the economy of Assam. The cane and bamboo units are likely to be of low-capital intensity, requiring inexpensive raw materials. The state is well known for large scale availability of cane and bamboo resources. Therefore, proper utilization and management of there resources will be able to increases the income level of the artisans. The cane and bamboo works are also normally associated with agriculture and provide subsidiary income to the rural people. Additional income benefits will be derived from the cane and bamboo works in the rural areas. During lean season of wet rice cultivation most of the rural people engage themselves in cane and bamboo works in order to utilized their surplus time. This supplements income level of the rural people in Assam. It is justifiably pointed out that our cane and bamboo works will play a significant role to increase per capita income, if we widely recognize the economic potentialities of cane and bamboo works with some positive measures in the state. In this connection it is to be noted that in the major cane and bamboo producing countries of South and South-east Asia (China, India, Indonesia and Philippines), half a million people formally works in cane based activates and over 2 million people in bamboo works. This work is often seasonal and viewed as a source of supplementary income of the people. It is estimated that the value of production of cane and bamboo industry was Rs. 259.70 lakhs in 1998-99 and it increased to Rs. 336.65 lakhs in 1999-2000 in the state.[8] The increasing value of cane and bamboo production also indicates that prospects of cane and bamboo works as remunerative enterprise in Assam is bright. Apart from the income generating justification, the cane and bamboo units help to bring about even distribution of income to the people by supplement the income to the poor people.

6.2.3. Earning Foreign Exchange:

The cane and bamboo works can play a significant role in earning foreign exchange for our country. The development of cane and bamboo works can also make best use of earning foreign exchange for Assam also. Because many items of this handicrafts have a good demand in many other countries. As per the Assam Government Marketing Corporation the knitted laxmi flower vase, jewellery box, square flower vase, jewellery box, square planter, half salads bowl, hanger, egg shape basket, stick type basket, fruit basket, gamla basket, round cylindrical planter, knitting fleered basket, round knitting basket, eight angle cane watch, knitting tray with handle, round knitting tray, half salad bowl, square fleered planter, triangular umbrella stand, round, hanging shade, round umbrella stand, round tray, square fleered umbrella stand, baby mini furniture, knitting bucket, bucket basket, sylindrical glanter, Kolochi murrah, mini baby jhula, sinhasan chair, mayur chair garden chair, sofa set, drining chair, baby cot etc. are exportable cane items of the state[9]. The Indian Institute of Foreign Trade (IIFT), New Delhi prepared a study on "Export Development Plan for Assam" in 2004 where bamboo and bamboo based products were identified as prospective exportable items. Moreover, it is also observed that the bamboo products like globe flower vase, round flower vase, furity tray, six angle double netting lamp, vegetable basket duble netting basket, tea tray, coffee tray, house lamp cup candle stand, round table lamp, dhol lamp, bowl lamp, salt sacker, oval show piece, peacock, magazine rack oval flower basket, ashtrays flower pachi plain pachi, duli set etc. are also having a good export potential in Assam. Besides, the cane and bamboo product have got substantial demand inside and outside the state. For example, Assam earned Rs 4.5 lakhs by selling cane baskets in the exhibitions held in Kolkota, Delhi and Mumbai in the year 1981. A substantial amount of income including valuable foreign exchanges are earned by the artisans of Assam by exporting the cane and bamboo items. It is to be noted that worldwide, per year domestic trade and subsistent use of cane and bamboo are accounted to be worth USD 2.5 billion and USD 4.5 billion respectively. Global exports of cane and bamboo generate another USD 4 billion and USD 2.7 billion respectively. It is observed that quality cane and bamboo products never face marketing problems and naturally these products are also supposed to have a huge potential market in the country and outside the country. Therefore, effective steps should be taken by cane and bamboo artisans to produce quality products and emphasis should be laid on export promotion to generate demand for the products in foreign countries.

6.2.4. Suitable for Sustainable Development:

It is known fact that degradation of the environment is a global problem in modern society. In the time of environmental degradation the cane and bamboo resources are considered as sustainable eco-friendly industrial materials of the future. The cane and bamboo resources fall into renewable natural resources. As we know that economic development cannot be sustained without preservation of the environment. The sustainability is currently one of the most important issues pertaining to development and environmental preservation. It is justifiably hoped that the setting of cane and bamboo units will play a significant role for sustainable development of the state economy. Cane and bamboo resources should be used by the artisans in such a manner that artisans activity should not lead to losses of rich biodiversity in the state. Awareness should be created among the people about the prospects of handicrafts sector by utilizing cane and bamboo resources for sustainable development. It may be mentioned that not only Assam but also in the whole of North Eastern region, the cane and bamboo units have been suitability placed for prospects of sustainable development. A technical report[10] published by NEHHDC has mentioned that N-E region can expect a quantum leap towards economic development in a sustainable way and etch out a name in the international arena of cane and bamboo. The cane and bamboo is a future prospect materials for this craft and needs to be handled with great care for economic development in sustainable way and sensitivity to provide better quality of life of the artisans of the state.

6.2.5. Entrepreneurship Development:

Entrepreneurship development has made significant contribution in providing income and employment to millions of peoples. In view of the above contributions, entrepreneurship development through cane and bamboo enterprise has come to occupy an important role in the economic progress of the state. The state also has potential for developing cane and bamboo entrepreneurship on the basis of local resources. It is of course true that there is a lack of entrepreneurial motivation of the Assamese people for which local enterprises are lagging behind in requirement, necessary for establishing cane and bamboo units. It is to be noted that in India, entrepreneurship development has been accepted as a strategy for achieving the twin objectives of promoting entrepreneurship, particularly among the educated unemployed youth and also for rapid industrialization[11]. Assam has also been accepted in the same strategy for entrepreneurship development as accepted in the country. As the state is famous for its own cane and bamboo resources, proper utilization and managements of these valuable renewable resources will be able to develop a large number of cane and bamboo based enterprises which will help generate employment and income opportunity in the state. In this context, the unemployed persons can take up the initiative for establishing cane and bamboo units. Guidance, encouragement and resources may not probably be a constraint for cane and bamboo entrepreneurship. The organizations like CBTC, NEDFi, AGMC, ARTFED, NEHHDC, KVIB, IIE, DC(H), DICC, etc. have been providing training facilities, financial help, market information and other inputs to promote entrepreneurship for cane and bamboo in the state. The industrial policy of the state government 2003, has identified cane and bamboo based industries as thrust areas. The IIT Guwahati is engaged in developing design for bamboo items to meet competition in the different part of the world. The Rain Forest Research Institute (RFRI) at Jorhat has recognized the role of cane and bamboo in the economic upliftment of the N-E region. The scientists of the RFRI has identified cane and bamboo as the most important species of the N-E region which will act as catalyst in poverty alleviation and stimulate industrial revolution[12]. It is encouraging to note that a special project for bamboo development was announced by the Prime Minister in India on World Environment Day in June 1999. It is to be noted that while inaugurating a craft village project for N-E region at Guwahati on 17th January 2006 Prime Minister Dr. Manmohan Singh said that this shilpogram represents the beauty and grace of the people of the N-E region of our country. It also captures the immense potential of the N-E region which, if properly harnessed with significantly improved economic and social conditions of the people[13]. Taking into consideration all the promotional and protective factors together there is a strong prospect for cane and bamboo entrepreneurship development in the economy of Assam. In this context, it is to be noted that the people can easily take advantage of the recent changes and supports offered by the government and concerning organizations for cane and bamboo entrepreneurship development in the economy of Assam.

It is clear from the above discussion that in spite of having some problems for development of cane and bamboo works, the prospects of these works are also bright in the state. The highly potential cane and bamboo industry should be developed in such a manner such a manner that it can attain the economic viability at its earliest and will also help in preserving the social, cultural and religious heritage of the people of Assam. It is also equally true that the future prospects will depend on raw materials, capital, labour, organization, entrepreneurship and economic facilities development. The cane and bamboo industry can rarely succeed unless it is able to weave together diverse support, promotion and protection from common endeavour. In the context of present liberalized economy, time has come for the entrepreneurs to realize the hard economic reality ensuring efficiency which is the key to the survival of the cane and bamboo units. The present scenario needs to be changed. The government and non-government agencies with appropriate programmes and projects can be help in proper utilization of renewable cane and bamboo resources for making the value added products in an eco-friendly way in Assam

References

1. *Assam Handicrafts Survey*, Small Industry Extension Training Institute, North East Regional Branch, Guwahati, 1982, p. 2.

2. *Report of Advisory Committee on Industry*, Vol. II, Assam, 1996, Annexure, p. 3.

3. Ibid, p. 4.

4. *District Industrial Centre and Commerce, Sivasagar District*, Sivasagar, Govt. of Assam, 2000.

5. *District Industrial Centre and Commerce, Jorhat District*, Jorhat, Govt. of Assam, 1999.

6. *Assam District Gazetteers, Lakhimpur District*, Govt. of Assam, Guwahati, 1976, p. 255.

7. *Development of Bamboo and Cane Sector in India*, Ministry of Environment and Forest, Govt. of India, New Delhi, 1999, p. 13.

8. *Statistical Hand Book, Assam*, 2001, Directorate of Economics and Statistics, Govt. of Assam, Guwahati, pp. 124-125.

9. *Assam's Sublime Handicrafts*, Assam Government Marketing Co-operations Ltd., Govt. of Assam, Guwahati, 2003.

10. *Study of Cane and Bamboo Reserve in North East India*, Technical Report, North Eastern Handicrafts and Handloom Development Corporation, Shillong, 2001, p. 66.

11. Mali, D.D., "A Case for Entrepreneurship Education," *Journal of North Eastern Council,* Vol. 21, No. 1, Shillong, 2001, p. 14.

12. Prasad, Krishna Govind., Bamboo Sector Development in the North East: Challenges and Opportunities, National Workshop on *Policy and Legal Issues in Cultivation and Utilization of Bamboo, Rattan and Forest Tress in Private and Community Land*, 7-9 August 2001, Kerals Forest Research Institute, Peechi, 2001, p. 92.

13. Borah, K.C., Key Note Address in the UGC Sponsored National Level Seminar on *Present Status of Handicrafts in the North-Eastern Region* Held at Gargaon College, Simalguri, 3rd and 4th February, 2006.

7

Summary, Suggestions and Conclusion

In the preceding chapters, the present status of handicrafts and their economics with particular reference to cane and bamboo works in Assam have been analyzed based on our sample survey. An attempt has also been made to identify the problems and evaluate the prospects of cane and bamboo works in Assam. For our study, 131 cane and bamboo units (35 registered and 96 non-registered) were randomly selected from rural and urban areas of the seven districts of Assam. To supplement the primary data information were also collected from different official and non-official sources.

This last Chapter embodies a summary of the findings on the analysis, suggestions and conclusion emerging there-from. It is to be noted that the findings are relevant to sample units, although they shed considerable light on the handicrafts sector including cane and bamboo works in Assam in general.

The **Chapter I** is chiefly introductory in nature and includes the definition of handicrafts and the significance of cane and bamboo works in Assam. From the beginning of the known human history, handicrafts form a valuable social, cultural and economic trait of a community. It is seen that the cane and bamboo crafts bear the witness of many cultures, traditions, races and civilization and these have been preserved by the long experience of skilled artisans of Assam. At present also the cane and bamboo products are part and parcel of the life of the people of the state. The introducing chapter includes the definition of handicrafts, importance of the study, objectives, hypothesis, methodology and research design and layout of the study.

The **Chapter II** has objectively examined the historical development including the present status of handicrafts in our country in general and our state in particular. It is observed that the study of the historical development of handicrafts is an essential key to the understanding of the peoples' culture. The traditions of many crafts in our country can trace their origins back to the ancient Indus valley and Mohenjo-Daro civilization. The artisans became an integral part within the social, economic and religions fabric of the way of life in medieval period. However, Indian handicrafts had not a received proper treatment in the hands of British government. The revival of cultural heritage of crafts were made part of the national freedom movement in India. In Assam too handicrafts had occupied an important position on the society and economy since ancient times. History showed that the craftsmen could perform excellent skill in ancient and medieval Assam. The handicrafts in the state had reached a very high point of perfection under the Ahom kings. Like other parts of India, the traditional crafts started declining under the British government in the state. The freedom movement gave an opportunity for artisans to work again and create artistic activity of crafts in Assam. Considering the importance of handicrafts for providing employment and income opportunities, both central and state governments have taken various steps for development of handicrafts. The AKVIB, KVIC, DICC, AGMC, ARTFED, NEHHDC, DC(H), ASIDC, CBTC etc., have taken the responsibility of various measures for the development of handicrafts in Assam. The DC(H) estimated that total number of handicrafts units and artisan were 30363 and 100482 in Assam in 1995-96. About sixteen craftsmen have received the prestigious National Award from 1966 to 1998 on different crafts for their excellent performance of handicrafts articles in the state. The budgetary support in Assam increased from Rs. 8.16 lakhs in 1997-98 to Rs. 21.90 lakhs in 1999-2000. It is observed that in spite of the rich heritage of handicrafts the handicrafts industry has not been able to fully develop professionally, at on expected level due to lack of proper infrastructural facilities in Assam. Considering the view that the handicrafts artisans are important elements for the economic development of Assam in the Tenth Five year plan is to provide adequate infrastructural facilities for setting up handicrafts units in Assam.

In the **Chapter III** review of existing relevant literature on various aspects of the handicrafts published at national and state levels. A few important studies on handicrafts in Assam are given here. S.N. Sarma (1967) has investigated the role of Satra institutions in the development of various crafts in Assam and observed the significant role. Amalendu Guha (1984) undertook an important study to discuss the crafts and technology system in the medieval period of Assam and expressed the view that simple bamboo and wooden implements were used in most of the crafts at that time. D.D. Mali (1989) has discussed the present status of handicrafts in Assam through a planned process. R.K. Saikia (2000) has discussed the decline of the traditional handicrafts during the British period of Assam. R. Gopalkrishran (2000) has made on attempt to analyse the present problems of handicrafts in Assam. It is observed from the overall review that there is a lack of a comprehensive analysis in the handicrafts sector in Assam. In fact, no fact finding works on handicrafts are available in the state. This fact strengthens the need for further intensive study toward filling up this gap.

The **Chapter IV** is divided into two sections. In **Section I** the socio-economic profile of the sample districts have been discussed. It is found that about 90.76 percent of population was living in rural areas in the Sivasagar district as per census 2001. The literacy rate was 75.33 percent and about 43.33 percent of workers were engaged in agriculture in the district in 2001. Oil and tea is the major industry of the district. The per capita gross domestic product was Rs. 21779.00 in 2000-01 in the district. Tinsukia district has recorded 80.53 percent of rural and 19.47 percent urban population as per census 2001. The literacy rate was 63.28 percent and about 37.37 percent total workers were engaged in agriculture in the district in 2001. Tea, oil and coal are the main industries of the district. The per capita gross domestic product has been found Rs. 17707.00 of the district in the year 2000-01. The central district, Nagaon had 12.02 percent of urban and 87.98 percent of rural population according to 2001 census. The literacy rate was 62.28 percent and nearly 58.28 percent of workers were engaged in agriculture in the district as per census 2001. The district is industrially backward relating to other districts of Assam. The per capita gross district domestic product was estimated Rs. 8081.00 in the year of 2000-01. The Nalbari district was inhabited by 97.61 percent rural and 2.39 percent urban population as per census 2001. The literacy rate was 68.08 percent and total 70.45 percent of workers were engaged in agriculture in the district according to census report 2001. The district is not developed industrially. The per capita gross domestic product was Rs. 8169.00 in the district in the year 2000-01. The north bank district of Sonitpur was accounted for 89.54 percent rural and 10.46 percent of urban population as per census 2001. The literacy rate was 60.29 percent and about 46.69 percent of workers were engaged in agriculture in the district in 2001. The district is also backward in respect of industrial development. The per capita gross district domestic product was Rs. 8323.00 in the year 2000-01. The capital city being located in the Kamrup district where the highest urban population (36%) was observed. The literacy rate was 74.69 percent and total 33.63 percent workers were engaged in agriculture in the district in 2001. The district is fast growing in industrial importance in Assam. The per capita gross district domestic product was Rs. 22292.00 in 2000-01. Goalpara district was sheltered by about 91.86 percent of rural population as per census 2001. The literacy rate was 58.56 percent; about 55.20 percent of workers were engaged in agriculture in the district. The district is one of the industrially backward in Assam. The per capita gross district domestic product was Rs. 62140.00 in 2000-01.

Section II of **Chapter IV** analyses the socio-economic conditions of the sample entrepreneurs of the cane and bamboo units covered under our sample based on certain socio-economic parameters. It also compares and contrasts the socio-economic status of the rural and urban sample entrepreneurs of the cane and bamboo units in our study areas. It is found from the analysis that the majority of 51.91 percent sample units were established between 1991-2001. About 45.35 percent of working rural units were established between 1991-2001, while 64.44 percent units in urban areas were established during this period. It reflects the fact that commercialism of cane and bamboo works in urban areas of Assam was started only during the last decade of the last century. It is found that total 97.67 percent rural sample units are under proprietorship and the rest 2.33 percent are partnership concern. In contrast, all urban sample units are operating under proprietorship. Proprietorship concern is the most popular form among the sample units. It is reported that the economic reason was the main factor for starting the cane and bamboo units in our study. About 67.44 percent rural and 97.78 urban entrepreneurs reported that economic reason is the basic motivating factor for establishing cane and bamboo works. Most of the rural entrepreneurs' family background is agriculture, where majority of the urban entrepreneurs family background is service and business. The majority of 41.98 percent sample entrepreneurs in both rural and urban areas were unemployed prior to entering to cane and bamboo works as their occupation. About 40 percent entrepreneurs were engaged in different type of petty business, in urban areas, where as 11.63 percent entrepreneurs reported in this activities in rural areas. It is found that 31.40 percent rural entrepreneurs have their previous occupation as cultivator. Almost similar pattern of male-female ratio of our surveyed units for rural and urban areas his found. The average family size worked out to be 5.03 of the sample entrepreneurs, is lower then the state average of 6.5. The participation of women in cane and bamboo enterprise has been very low in comparison to men. Only 4.44 percent woman entrepreneurs were found in urban areas. The majority of (89.31 %) rural entrepreneurs are married. In contrast, 87.21 percent entrepreneurs are married in urban areas. So far as educational levels of the sample entrepreneurs are concerned about 90.70 percent rural sample entrepreneurs and about 53.33 percent urban entrepreneurs are found below HSLC level. Only 4.45 percent entrepreneurs are found to be graduate in urban areas. But none is found graduate in rural areas. The dominant age group of the sample entrepreneurs is 31 to 45 years in both rural and urban areas. The structure of the majority units (66.28 %) are katcha in rural areas. In contrast, 51.11 percent units have semi-pacca structure in urban areas. Only 12.98 percent units have pacca structure in both rural and urban areas. Significantly, only 2.33 percent rural units have electricity connection as against 46.67 percent urban units. Only 11.11 percent sample units have telephone facilities is urban areas. All rural sample units have employed untrained workers for cane and bamboo works. Only 4.44 percent sample entrepreneurs have employed trained workers in urban areas. Two third of the rural units are engaged in producing almost all the items, where as in case of urban areas one third produce all types of cane and bamboo items. Furniture and decorative items are absent in rural units. The survey reveals that more than half of the units surveyed in rural areas do not maintain a particular marketing channel. The most important channel was found to be channel II (Sale at own units) in urban areas. There are existence of middlemen in marketing process in the rural areas where it is not found in urban areas.

It is seen that basics raw materials like cane, bamboo, ***takou leaf*** etc. are not available locally of all times for both rural and urban units. About 69.77 percent rural and 75.65 percent urban sample units have faced similar problems in getting regular supply of raw materials for their works. Regarding the credit, it was reported that the traders were common in supplying loan to the sample units particularly in rural areas. About 8.89 percent urban units have taken loan from nationalized banks. As the production technique is mostly traditional and operated in a small scale with no professional zeal the credit requirement in cane and bamboo crafts is less. This is revealed in our findings. About 26.74 percent rural and 68.89 percent urban sample entrepreneurs are in favour modern technology for cane and bamboo works in the study areas.

The discussion of economics of the cane and bamboo units covered by our survey is made in **Chapter V**. We observed that the manpower cost occupied the highest among the variable cost of the cane and bamboo crafts. So far as fixed cost is concerned, rent on building was found highest both for rural and urban units. (This is due to the fact that apportion of rent on building is made on the prevailing market rate). The average annual production cost for all the items produced in a year worked out to 71.69 percent and 28.31 percent for variable and fixed cost respectively for rural units. In contrast, total 64.44 percent is estimated as variable cost and the rest 35.56 percent is fixed cost for urban units. The survey reveals that as high as about 97 percent for the produce of the both rural and urban units have been sold and the rest remained as inventory annually. In the estimate of net income, it is seen that the average annual net income per unit both rural (Rs. 5063.77) and urban (Rs. 6472.82) areas are found to be highest in the Kamrup district, where as, it is lowest for both rural (Rs. 3257.16) and urban (Rs. 4541.37) units in Goalpara district. The average annual total income per units for both rural (Rs. 22417.07) and urban (Rs. 35108.45) are found to be the highest in Kamrup district. The average number of family workers per unit is highest (4.08) in Tinsukia district and the lowest (2.10) in the Nagaon district in the rural units. In contrast, the average number of family workers per unit is the highest (3.25) in the Nalbari district and the lowest (1.56) in the Sivasagar district for urban units. The income of per family workers is the highest for both rural (Rs. 4528.36) and urban (Rs.8820.58) units in the Sivasagar district. Inter -district inequalities have been observed in respect of average annual net income per unit from cane and bamboo works in our study areas. In our findings it was observed that in additions to the cane and bamboo works, entrepreneurs earned other income from difference sources. All rural sample units have earned income from agriculture and allied activities. About 80 percent of urban units earn income from different types of petty business. The average annual per unit income from all sources was found highest for rural in the Kamrup district (Rs. 35582.16) and the lowest in the Goalpara district (Rs. 29560.95). The average per capita income is Rs. 6410.45 and Rs. 9372.78 respectively for rural and urban units. Average per capita income from all sources was found lower for rural in Goalpara district, where as for urban units the per capita income was found highest (Rs.

12542.85) in Sonitpur district. In comparison of per capita income of sample units with that of the state average, it was found that in our findings it is lower than the state average.

Attempt was also made to find out the break-even point of the units covered by our survey and it was found that the P/V ration , BEP (in terms of sale) and margin of safety of the rural units 35.51 percent, Rs. 23932.84 and Rs. 9444.22 respectively. In contrast, the P/V ratio, BEP(in terms of sale) and margin of safety of the urban units is 39.86 percent, Rs.44300.63 and Rs. 8920.99 respectively.

Chapter VI examines the problems of cane and bamboo works and identifies the prospects of this works in the state. This chapter is divided into two sections. In **Section I**, while studying the major problems faced by the cane and bamboo units, it is observed that the sample cane and bamboo units are facing various problems while managing their business. Here, problems are ranked it has been given by the respondents. The rural sample entrepreneurs reported ten problems, where urban sample entrepreneurs reported six basic problems for cane and bamboo works in our study area. The lack of finance, stiff competition with other products, high cost of production, marketing problem, non-available of raw materials, lack of systematic guidance, inadequate transport and communication facilities, lack of proper training facilities, lack of new design of the product and excessive market levy, are reported by respondents as major problems for development of cane and bamboo works. In addition to these problems, other noteworthy problems which stand on the way of cane and bamboo works development in the state are: the frequent power failure, forced sale and lack of trained workers. The gap between demand and supply of cane and bamboo products adversely effects the growth and expansion of the cane and bamboo industry in the state. The sample units in many occasions could not utilize their capacity fully because of the problems mentioned above. It is to be noted that both central and state government established some agencies like DC(H), NEHHDC, CTBT, AGMC, ARTFED, KVIC etc. for overall development of cane and bamboo works, but these agencies fail to achieve their objectives in this regard. It is being increasingly realized that it is essential on the part of agencies to reduce the basic infrastructural problems for the development of cane and bamboo works at priority level in Assam.

In **Section II,** the findings of the prospects of cane and bamboo works reveal that in spite of various problems that are faced by the cane and bamboo works in Assam the prospects of development of these works are bright. The limited capital investment, labour intensive method, use of local resources, inherent skill obtained by many rural people and export potential of the products indicate their suitability of cane and bamboo works in the economy of Assam. Apart from the above economic suitability, it is observed that the setting of cane and bamboo units will play a significant role for sustainability of important economic reasons. Moreover, it is expected that the entrepreneurship development through cane and bamboo enterprise will occupy an important role in the economic development in Assam. There are many cane and bamboo items in Assam which are in high demand in countries like USA, UK Japan and France. These products have good prospects for development through diversification and modernization process. The analysis of the existing scenario has revealed that the cane and bamboo works become more relevant from the angle of economics, culture, equality and eco-friendly in nature in Assam.

Suggestions:

The following promotional and protective measures are suggested for smooth growth and development of cane and bamboo works in the state of Assam.

7.1. In order to develop the cane and bamboo works the basic necessity is to create initiative by the government. The government may consider the giving of interest free loan to the master artisans. The requirement of security against the loan must be relaxed and the sanction and disbursement process should be simplified and quickened. The financial agencies should also come forward to reduce complex lending procedure and delay in taking decision for financing the cane and bamboo artisans.

7.2. Effort should be made to the supply of raw materials required for cane and bamboo works at reasonable rates to the artisans. For this purpose the state government may consider the possibility of establishing raw materials depot in every district of the state. The existing cane and bamboo units shall be allotted adequate quantity of raw materials from this depot so that artisans utilize their full capacity. Moreover, treatment, processing and preservation process of raw materials are to be taught to the artisans.

7.3. The transport and communication system has its own contribution in making a market system developed and efficient. In order to promote the cane and bamboo crafts, transport and communication system should be developed to link villages with different markets and to link village markets with the town markets in the state. In this connection, the state government should also encourage private participation in transport and communication network in the state.

7.4. The establishment of cane and bamboo co-operative societies can solve many of the major problems like new design, finance, supplying raw materials, marketing of the products etc. The government can do much by providing cheap credit facility, marketing support and supply of quality raw materials through the co-operative societies to the cane and bamboo artisans. The co-operative coverage is very little in cane and bamboo crafts. If co-operatives are formed than it will be possible also in the elimination of middlemen.

7.5. The design of products of cane and bamboo works must be improved and changed as per the changing of tastes and preferences of consumers. Thus, it is highly essential to give due weight for design development in cane and bamboo works. Design development workshop and seminars are required to be organized in different part of the state with the help of the experts from National Institute of Design, Ahmedabad, Industrial Design Centre, IIT, Mumbai, Bamboo and Cane Development Institute (BCDI), Agartala and other such concerning organizations. Improved tools and equipments are to be provided to the artisans to produce new design cane and bamboo items.

7.6. It is observed that population growth, practice of jhum cultivation, small tea plantation and industrialization are the main factors for reducing the cane and bamboo forest areas in the state. Thus, in new areas quick growing cane and bamboo cultivation should be encouraged and supported in the line of plantation crop such as rubber, coffee and tea in Assam. The forest department of Assam should make special programmes for the cultivation and preservation of cane and bamboo. The state government may consider the possibility for setting up a Cane and Bamboo Board for cultivation, conservation and protection of cane and bamboo species in Assam.

7.7. The handicrafts organizations like AGMC, DC(H), NEHHDC should increase the schemes and programmes of marketing workshops, fairs, expos, exhibitions and set up craft bazaars. Beside, can and bamboo products sale emporia must be opened in all important towns. Market information should be provided to the cane and bamboo artisans through different media like radio, television and newspaper. The AGMC should make special efforts for purchasing of cane and bamboo products in the rural area of Assam. This corporation should take steps to introduce Mobile Crafts Exhibition of cane and bamboo items in the towns and cities in the countries as well as outside the country will help proper marketing of the products.

7.8. Training for the craftsmen should be an integral part of any cane and bamboo crafts development programme. In order to create quality items, systematic training should be provided to the artisans on latest design development and application of modern techniques of production in the cane and bamboo works. The DICCs, NEHHDC, DC (H), AGMC, CBTC etc. can arrange basic training selected artisans and special training to master artisans by providing scholarships, free boarding and lodging. The government should also take steps with collaboration of NGOs to organize refresher courses, orientation courses and workshops for the cane and bamboo artisans.

7.9. The export potentiality of cane and bamboo to the foreign countries products is growing, in the context of economic liberalization. Both the public and private sectors have their role to play in the export of cane and bamboo items. For exporting of cane and bamboo products, systematic efforts should be made about product identification, supply arrangement, price, delivery, payment and quality of products. The state governments may be consider to open Export Centres for exportable cane and bamboo items in the major cities like Delhi, Mumbai and Kolkata in the country. The concerning handicrafts organizations should also take steps to make advertisements and propaganda to popularize the exportable items inside and outside the country. The NEHHDC, AGMC, DC(H) etc. should take the lead being associated with the Handicrafts and Handlooms Export Corporation (HHEC) and the Handicrafts Export Promotion Council (HEPC) to export the cane and bamboo products from Assam.

7.10. In our study we observed that majority of the cane and bamboo entrepreneurs are elder. The younger generations do not seem attracted towards this crafts. Therefore, intensive facilities need to be extended to the technically qualified and other educated young men in the better run cane and bamboo works in the state. The facilities like loan subsidies, tax exemption, raw materials, tools etc. have to be extended by the government. It is felt that if the qualified local young men of the state come forward with their active initiative for the establishment of different type of cane and bamboo units, it will help increasing production, generating employment and income in both rural and urban people in the state.

7.11. There should be a separate directorate at the state level for handicrafts in Assam to carry out plans and programmes in order to provide incentive to local entrepreneurs over expansion and modernization of all existing crafts including cane and bamboo crafts.

7.12. The cane and bamboo works need the policy support from unfair competition, from the state government. It is also necessary to, supply of electricity at a consessional rate, to provide subsidy and insurance benefit for cane and bamboo works in the state.

7.13. The government may consider to import improved tools and machines from craft developed countries like Japan, China and Malaysia for the development of cane and bamboo works in Assam. Efforts should be made for the arrangement of study-visits of cane and bamboo artisans to different parts in India and foreign countries. The arrangement of such study-visits will provide an opportunity to the cane and bamboo artisans to learn new process of works and to learn the new methods of production.

Professionalism should be created among the cane and bamboo artisans in the state.

7.14. There is lack of in-depth research, either by individual or by government research institutions to know the problems and prospects of cane and bamboo works in the state. It is increasingly felt that availability of reliable statistical data is the pre condition to comprehensive planning for future development of cane and bamboo works. Therefore, it is necessary to undertake comprehensive research on present status and future prospect of cane and bamboo works in Assam by individual researchers or government agencies.

Conclusion

The future development of handicrafts in Assam, particularly of cane and bamboo works will be governed by the extent of basic infrastructural facilities and their proper utilization, appropriate government policy and entrepreneurial motivation of the young men. Keeping in view the consumers' preference and stiff competition of plastic items, there is a need of producing value added items, which will not only provide employment and income to crafts persons, but will also help in preserving the social and cultural heritage of the Assamese people. It is sincerely hoped that the present study will draw the attention of planners and policy makers in the state. It is further hoped that our study will open a door to the researchers to pursue research at the micro level, covering all the aspects of disperse cane and bamboo units. We hopes that promotional and protective steps be taken by all concerned to develop the handicrafts industry in such a manner that the handicrafts industry will be able to develop professionally which can provide economically-viable occupation to thousands of people of Assam.

Appendices

Appendix – I
Name of the Cane Species in Assam

Sl. No.	*Botanical Name*	*Local Name*
1	*Calamus leptospadix*	Lejai
2	*Calamus tenuis*	Jatibet
3	*Calamus latifolius*	Horna bet
4	*Calamus nambariensis*	Houka
5	*Calamus khasianus*	
6	*Calamus gracilis*	Chulibet
7	*Calamus flagellum*	Raidang
8	*Calamus erectus*	Jeng
9	*Calamus floribundus*	Lejai
10	*Calamus acanthospathus*	Jati
11	*Calamus guruba*	Sundibet
12	*Calamus kingianus*	-

(Contd.)

(Contd. Appendix-I)

Sl. No.	*Botanical Name*	*Local Name*
13	*Calamus sp.*	-
14	*Daemsonorop jenkinsianus*	Golla bet, Raidang
15	*Daemonorops sp.*	Golla bet, Raidang
16	*Plectocomia assamica*	Hatibet, Raja bet
17	*Plectocomia bractealis*	Panibet
18	*Zalacca secunda*	Jeng

Source: Study of Cane and Bamboo Reserve in North East India, Technical Report, North Eastern Handicrafts and Handloom Development Corporation, Shillong, 2001.

Appendix – II

Name of the Bamboo Species in Assam

Sl. No.	*Scientific Name*	*Local Name*
1	*Bambusa auriculata*	Kalia banh
2	*Bambusa bambos*	Kotoha, Kotabah
3	*Bambusa balcooa*	Bhaluka
4	*Bambusa jaintiana*	-
5	*Bambusa mastersii*	Beti Banh
6	*Bambusa nutans*	Deobanh, Jotia makal
7	*Bambusa pallida*	Bijuli, Jowa Mukal
8	*Bambusa polymorpha*	Betua, Jama
9	*Bambusa pseudopallida*	-
10	*Bambusa teres*	Bhaluki makal, Paura
11	*Bambusa tulda*	Jati, Nal banh
12	*Bambusa vulgaris*	Tansti banh, Ketura
13	*Bambusa sp.*	Nangal banh
14	*Dendrocalamus giganteus*	Worra
15	*Dendrocalamus hamiltonii*	Kakoa, Kakeo banh
16	*Dendrocalamus strictus*	Karail, Jati
17	*Dendrocalamus longispathus*	Karail, Jati, Rupahi banh
18	*Dinochloa compactiflora*	-
19	*Dinochloa gracilis*	-
20	*Dinochloa indica*	-
21	*Dinochloa mclellandii*	Lota
22	*Gigantochloa albociliata*	Kalisundi
23	*Gigantochloa macrostachya*	-

(Contd.)

(Contd. Appendix-II)

Sl. No.	*Scientific Name*	*Local Name*
24	*Melocanna baccifera=M.bambusoides*	Tarai banh, Nah banh, Muli banh
25	*Phyllostachys assamica*	-
26	*Schizostachyum dullooa*	Dalu banh
27	*Schizostachyum griffithii*	Behti banh
28	*Schizostachyum pergracile*	Madang
29	*Schizostachyum polymorphum*	Bajaj banh

Source: Study of Cane and Bamboo Reserve in North East India, Technical Report, North Eastern Handicrafts and Handloom Development Corporation, Shillong, 2001.

Appendix – III
Survey Schedule
(Part = 1)

Block = 1: Units Particulars.

1. Units no :
2. Owner of the Units :
3. Religion :
4. Qualification :
5. Community :
6. District :
7. Block :
8. Sub-Division :
9. Village :
10. Town :
11. Registered :
12. Non Registered :

BLOCK = II: Demographic Particulars.

Sl. No	*Religion with the head of the family*	*Age*	*Sex*	*Economic Status*	*Education Status*	*Remarks*
1						
2						
3						

BLOCK = III Occupation Distribution of Member of the Owner of the Unit

Sl. No	*Occupation Status*		*Annual man days engaged in Primary works*	*Annual man days engaged in Secondary Work*	*Total man days engaged*
	Primary	*Secondary*			
1					
2					
3					

BLOCK: IV : Land Particulars

Sl. No	*Types of Land*	*Total Area (Bigha)*	*Land Used for Cultivation (Bigha)*	*Land used for Homestead, Tank and Garden (Bigha)*	*Waste Land (Bigha)*	*Irrigation area (Bigha)*
1						
2						
3						

BLOCK: V : Particular of Crops Grown

Sl. No	*Crops*	*Preceding Year*		*Current Year*	
		Yield	*Total Yield*	*Yield*	*Total Yield*
1	Paddy				
2	Jute				
3	Sugar Cane				

BLOCK = VI : Structure of Unit

Sl No			
1	Year of the Establishment		
2	Type of unit		
		Kutcha	
		Semi Pucca	
		Pucca	
		Rental	
		Own	
3	Electricity		
4	Telephone		
5	Internet		
6	Total Works		Number
		Skilled	
		Unskilled	
		Total	
		Local	
		Outside of the state	
		Total	
7	Financial Status		Amount (Rs)
		Own Finance	
		Bank Loan Finance	

BLOCK = VII : Particular of Loan Finance

Sl. No	*Source*	*Preceding Year*				*Current Year*			
		Amount taken	*Rate of Interest*	*Terms of Payment*	*Amount paid*	*Amount taken*	*Rate of Interest*	*Terms of Payment*	*Amount paid*
1	Money Lenders								
2.	Traders								
3	Relative and Friend								
4	Co-operative Society								
5	Rural Bank								
6	Nationalized Bank								
7	Other Banks								
8	Others								

Block =VIII : Items Produced

Sl. No	*Particular*	*Per Month*	*Price*	*Per Year*	*Price*
1					
2					
3					

Block = IX: Particular of Sale

Sl No	*Preceding Year*		*Current Year*	
	Ordered	*Readymade*	*Ordered*	*Readymade*
1				
2				
3				

BLOCK = X Marketing Cost

Year	*Labour*	*Transport*	*Communication*	*Taxes*	*Others*	*Total market cost*
Preceding						
Current						

BLOCK = XI : Fixed capital (In Rs.)

Sl. No	*Particulars*	*Amount*	*Per Year*
1.	Land on Building		
2.	Furniture and Fixture		
3.	Others		

BLOCK = XII: Working Capital (In Rs.)

Sl. No.	*Particulars*	*Per Months*	*Per Year*
1.	Raw Materials		
2.	Manpower		
3.	Telephone and Postage		
4.	Correspondence		
5.	Internet		
6.	Electricity		
7.	Others		
Total			

BLOCK = XIII: Other Expenditure (In Rs.)

Sl. No.	*Particulars*	*Per Month*	*Per Year*
1.	Insurance		
2.	Contingencies		
3.	Others		

BLOCK = XIV: Particular of Cost of Production

SL. NO	*Items*	*Materials*	*No/Kg*	*Price (Rs.)*
1	One Murha	Bamboo		
		Cane		
		Human labour (Days)		
		Others		
2	A medium size of furniture (sofa)	Bamboo		
		Cane		
		Human labour (Days)		
		Others		

(Contd.)

(Contd. Block)

SL. NO	*Items*	*Materials*	*No/Kg*	*Price (Rs.)*
3	A Fulam Japi	Bamboo		
		Cane		
		Human labour (Days)		
		Others		
4	Mats	Bamboo		
		Cane		
		Human labour (Days)		
5	Others	Bamboo		
		Cane		
		Human labour (Days)		
		Others		

Block = XV : Particular of Products Sold

Sl. No	*Items*	*Preceding Years*		*Current Year*	
		No.	*Price (Rs.)*	*No.*	*Price (Rs.)*

Block = XVI: Other Income of the Owner (In Rs)

Sl.No	*Particulars*	*Per Month(Rs)*	*Per Year (Rs)*
1	Forestry		
2	Fishery		
3	Sericulture		
4	Poultry		

(Contd.)

(Contd. Block)

Sl.No	*Particulars*	*Per Month(Rs)*	*Per Year (Rs)*
5	Livestock		
6	Business (Specify)		
7	Wages and Salary Earning		
8	Others		
Total			

(Part -II)
Questionnaire to Respondent

1. What form organization of the unit?

1. Proprietorship.
2. Partnership.
3. Companies.
4. Co-operative.
5. Others.

2. Why cane and bamboo works been taken up?

   1. For earning livelihood.
   2. For its creativity .
   3. For a available raw materials.
   4. For its increasing demand
   5. Because of its hereditary.
   6. To spend leisure time.
   7. Others.

3. Do you have any problems in marketing of Cane and Bamboo Products? Yes/No If Yes, make the problems according to preference

    1. Lack of new Design.
    2. Market too far from the production centre.
    3. Lack of transport and communication facilities.
    4. Non arability of Government agency.
    5. Stiff competition with other products.

4. Please rank the main problems of Cane and Bamboo Works?

    1. Lake of finance.
    2. Non available of raw materials.
    3. High cost of production.
    4. Lack of proper training facilities.
    5. Design of the products.
    6. Absence of proper marketing facilities.
    7. Limited transport and communication facilities.
    8. Lack of Systematic guidance.
    9. Stiff competition with other products.
    10. Excessive market levy.

5. Favorable days for Works:-

    1. January to March
    2. April to June.
    3. July to September.
    4. October to December.

6. Please give your suggestion for the development of Cane Bamboo works.

Sl.No	
1	
2	
3	

7. Do you think that cane and bamboo works is suitable for the economy? Yes/No.

8. Are you aware that government has a number of scheme for cane and bamboo works.

   a. Fully aware

   b. Partially aware

   c. Not aware

9. Do you think that government scheme are effective. Yes/No

10. Is not what is you suggestions?

Sl.No	
1	
2	
3	

11. Have you availed of any government scheme? Yes/No

12. Have you availing credit from institutional agencies? Yes/No

13. Is not what is the reasons?

Sl. No	*Reason*
1	
2	
3	

14. Name of Local Species of cane and bamboo which are used for cane and bamboo works

    a. Cane

    b. Bamboo

15. In which sources of finance you have received credit for your unit.

16. Do you manage you own found? Yes/No

17. Do you feel that credit supplied is sufficient for you requirement? Yes/No.

18 Do you known of any source from which credits can be obtained? Yes/No.

19. Is other credits on? Yes/No

20. Do you feel that any problem is getting regular supply of raw materials? Yes/No.

21. Are you raw materials available locally? Yes/No.

22 Do you feel any problem in getting hired skilled labour? Yes/No

23. Are you hired skilled labour available locally? Yes/No.

24. Do you sale your products under any compulsion (force sale)? Yes/No

25. If yes what is you obligatory? Repayment loan/Advance taken/ others.

26. To whom do you sale you Products? Trader/Govt. Agency / Consumer/Middlemen/others.
27. Do you Produced on demand [Advanced payment]? Yes/No
28. If yes how many Produced you? No/Qty.
29. Are you aware of market prices of your products? Yes/No.
30. Do you think demand of cane and bamboo products have increased? Yes/No
31. What type of tools and instruments use for your work? Traditional/Modern.
32. Do you felt that importance of modern method of technique for cane and bamboo works.
33. Do you have any associations/ organizations? Yes/No
34. If yes at what capacity?
35. Are you a member of any artisan's associations/ organizations? Yes/No
36. Do you think that New Economic Policy adopted by the central government will be affected badly the cane and bamboo works in Assam? Yes/No.
37. Do you happy doing the cane and bamboo works? Yes/No
38. The unit is fully utilize installed capacity? Yes/No
39. If not what percent approximately?
40. Do you give training of unskilled workers. Yes/No.
41. Do you appoint training workers. Yes/No
42. If yes what number.

43. What type of your family background? Agriculture/ Business/Service holder/others.

44. What is your occupation before coming cane and bamboo works unemployed/working private organization/ business/others.

45. What was initial capital employed for Cane and Bamboo Works.

46. Do you get job satisfaction doing Cane and Bamboo Works.

47. Do you export your products outside the state.

48. Do you export your products outside the country.

49. Investigation's comments and observations.

(Part-III)
Official

1. Name of the DICC

2. Name of the respondent (officer)

3. Total number of registered can and bamboo units under DICC

   a. Rural

   b. Urban

4. Total number of non registered cane and bamboo units under DICC

   a. Rural

   b. Urban

5. Successful units under your office

Sl. No.	*Name*	*Owner*	*Place*
1.			
2.			
3.			

6. What are the items produced in the successful unit?
   a.
   b.
   c.
7. What type of service rendered to the successful unit?
   a. Training Facility
   b. Financial support
   c. Equipment supply
8. Do you think that government support is sufficient for cane and bamboo works?
9. What is you view about the cane and bamboo units under your office.
10. Any caner and bamboo products are exported under your centre? Yes/No
    If yes, what are products?
    a.
    b.
    c.
11. The Cane and Bamboo raw materials are available under your centre?
12. How many artisans have received the national award for developing new cane and bamboo products?
13. What is you suggestion for the development of cane and bamboo units?
    a.
    b.
    c.
    d.

14. Do you think that the future prospects of cane and bamboo works is bright?

15. Investigation Comments and observation?

Date:- Signature of the Investigator

Appendix IV
List of National Award Winners on Cane and Bamboo Crafts in the North Eastern States, 2002.

Sl. No.	*States*	*No. of total artisans*
1	Arunachal Pradesh	3
2	Assam	2
3	Manipur	1
4	Meghalaya	-
5	Mizoram	1
6	Nagaland	1
7	Tripura	17
Total	-	25

Source: NER, Handicrafts at a Glance, Office of the Development Commissioner (Handicrafts), Ministry of Textile, Govt. of India, Guwahati, 2002.

Appendix -V
List of Artisans National Award Winners in Assam During 1966-98

Sl.No	*Name*	*Craft*	*Year of award*
1	Late Hareswar Deka	Bell Metal	1966
2	Shri Rasik Chandra Dey	Sital Pati	1966
3	Shri Raj Mohan Das	Silal Pati	1968
4	Shri Saral Bala Devi	Terracotta	1982
5	Shri Bhagawan Ch. Deka	Brass and Bell Metal	1984
6	Shri Ajit Kr. Das	Kalamkari	1987
7	Shri Motor Karmakar	Dokra	1987
8	Shri Sadanada Das	Bamboo Craving	1987
9	Smt. Hri Uttar Deka	Weaving	1988
10	Smt. Apli Rabha	Weaving	1990
11	Smt. Lady Rabha	Weaving	1990
12	Smt Amaya Rabha	Weaving	1991
13	Miss Aprika Rabhabala	Weaving	1993
14	Mrs Parul Ardo	Tribal Dress Material	1993
15	Shri Madhab Biswas	Bamboo Craft	1997
16	Shri Monondra Deka	Cane and bamboo	1998

Source: NER, Handicrafts at a Glance, Office of the Development Commissioner (Handicrafts), Ministry of Textiles, Govt. of India, Guwahati, 2002

Appendix VI
List of Artisans State Awards in Handicrafts of Assam

Sl. No	*Name*	*Crafts*
1	Shri Mohendra Mohan	Cane and Bamboo
2	Shri Sadoor Hussain	Wood Carving
3	Shri Mahadev Paul	Terracotta
4	Smt. Sandhya Konwar	Wood Carving
5	Shri Ron Neog	Cane Production
6	Shri Bhagawan Ch. Deka	Bell Metal
7	Mrs. Bhadrawati Das	Decorative Textiles
8	Shri Gopesh Deka	Bell Metal

Source: Assam, Handicrafts at a Glance, NER, Office of the Development Commissioner (Handicrafts) Ministry of Textile, Govt. of India, Guwahati, 2000

Appendix -VII
List of Artisans Merit certificate Winners of Assam

Sl. No	*Name*	*Districts*
1	Shri Rameswar Haziraka	Sonitpur
2	Shri Iambodhar Hazarika	Sonitpur
3	Shri Baneswar Neog	District name is not available
4	Shri Aman Ali	Bangaigaon
5	Shri Kalpanath Bhuan	Barpeta
6	Shri Sailendra Nath Das	Barpeta
7	Shri Digendra Mohan Das	Cachar
8	Smt. Lakhi Prabha Bordoloi	Jorhat
9	Shri Nitya Biswas	Nogaon
10	Shri Ashit Paul	Nagaon
11	Shri Khagendra Nath Deka	Nalbari
12	Shri Sardbeswar Das	Nalbari
13	Shri Adya Ranjan Borthakur	Dibugarh
14	Shri Dulav ch. Sarmah	Dibugarh
15	Shri Ananda Saikia	Jorhat
16	Shri Manab Dev Raja	Jorhat
17	Shri Guneswar Boro	Kamrup
18	Shri Amarjit Sinha	Kamrup
19	Shri Bholanath Paul	Dhubri

Source: Assam, Handicrafts at a Glance, NER, Office of the Development Commissioner (Handicrafts), Ministry of Textile Govt. of India, Guwahati, 2000

Appendix – VIII
Measures Suggested for the Development of Handicrafts Sector by Advisory Committee on Industry

Short Term Measures :

1. The artisans in the Handicrafts Sector are mostly in the un-organized sector: Efforts should be made by the Govt. to organize these artisans so that viable units are produced.
1. Availability of raw-materials is the main problems for the artisans. Cane and Bamboo has become a rare commodity. Whatever is available the price is exorbitant. Similar is the case of Copper and Zinc for the Bell Metal Producing artisans. A central store can be established by ASIDC which will supply the inputs at reasonable rates to the artisans and SSI units. Kerosine is an important input where Cane & Bamboo Handicrafts are concerned. The SSI units engaged in it are not supplied Kerosine at Government administered prices and they are to buy it from the open market. Supply Department may be requested to issue permits to all SSI units so engaged.
2. Transformation of finished products for the Handicrafts is vary erratic. Though the normal procedure is to book them through railway there are

several drawbacks. Delay in delivery is one problem, theft and pilferage is another. Besides orders are received often from places which do not have a nearby rail head. As such, products are often to be sent by road transport and the transporters charges very high rates. They also insists on a bulk truch load charge, even if the quantity is far less. Matter may be taken up with Railway Authority and Transport Department to help these SSI units.

3. Like the National Handloom Expo held annually for the promotion of Handlooms with 20% rebate, exhibition of Handicrafts should also be held at different Metropolitan cities and towns of India. This will give a boots to the marketing problems faced by the artisans.
4. The export promotion Council for Handicrafts, New Delhi, holds annual Handicrafts and Gift fare exhibition but it changes about Rs. 30,000/- for a single stall in the exhibition. This should be minimized.

Long Term Measures.

1. Social Forestry Department should go for Bamboo and Cane plantation so that the artisans can find their raw-material locally at a reasonable price.
2. ASIDC should strengthen their raw-material division so that SSI units can find any raw-material they want locally.
3. There should be a ban on Cane and Bamboo regarding movement outside the State.

Source: Advisory Committee on Industry, Assam, Vol, II, 1996

Appendix – IX
(Definitions)

1. Rural Unit:- A rural unit situated in village area.
2. Urban Unit:- An urban unit situated in town or city area.
3. Fixed Cost:- Furniture and instrument, rent on building, depreciation and interest on fixed cost are included in fixed cost.
4. Variable Cost:- Cost such as manpower cost, raw materials, marketing cost, interest on working capital, telephone, electricity, postal, training of worker cost etc.
5. Method of computing depreciation:- Twenty percent depreciation of all tools and machines using cane and bamboo units in a year is calculated.
6. Human Labour:- Family labour plus Hired labour = Total labour. Actural amount paid in cash and kind to casually hired labourers; the payment made in cash and kind as wage to the permanently hired labour (estimated on the basis of number of days devoted to cane and bamboo works separately), and the labour day devoted to cane and bamboo works

by the family labour evaluated at the rate paid to casually hired labour are estimated in labour charge. Conversion: All human labour worked in the cane and bamboo units have been converted into man-day, i.e., 8 hour man-day = 1 man day

7. Evaluation of rent: - Rent on building is evaluated at the price prevailing in the village and town.
8. Evaluation of cane and bamboo products:- The value of cane and bamboo products are estimated on the basis of the selling prices as reported by the respondents.
9. Full-time worker:- A full time worker is one who worker on the cane and bamboo for 8 hours in a day.
10. Part-time worker: A part time worker is one who works on the cane and bamboo for less than 8 hours in a day.
11. Income from cane and bamboo Works:- This income earned by an entrepreneur from the cane and bamboo works.
12. Other Sources of income:- This income earned by an entrepreneurs from agriculture and allied works or petty business that supplements main sources of income.
13. Income from all sources:- Income earned by an entrepreneur from cane and bamboo works and agriculture and allied works or petty business in a year.
14. Level of Income:- The level of income earned by an entrepreneur meaning the range between the maximum and minimum level of income earned by the entrepreneur.
15. Interest charge:- Five present interest charge for fixed and variable capital used in cane and bamboo works are calculated in a year.

16. Net Income:- Gross income to entrepreneur minus total cost.

Per unit income from Can and Bamboo:- Gross income minus production cost = Net income + Family labour cost + rental value.

Glossary

1. Bahi : A Flute
2. Bichani : Fan
3. Bor-chunga : A kind of weaving instrument
4. Bar-pira : Platform used for sitting
5. Chepa : A kind of fish-trap
6. Chalani : Sieve
7. Charakee : A kind of weaving instrument
8. Cheri : A kind of weaving instrument
9. Dola : Tray
10. Doon : Measure
11. Dhara : Mat
12. Dhanu : A kinds of instrument used for hunting
13. Duli : Big basket
14. Dula : A kind of litter
15. Dingaru : A kind of fish trap
16. Gagona : A kind of musical instrument
17. Garaka : A kind of weaving instrument
18. Garu Ason : A kind of small wooden stand installed at prayer hall
19. Hali : A kind of weaving instrument’

20.	Hukuma	:	A kind of fish-trap
21.	Japi	:	Hat
22.	Jakoi	:	A kind of fish-trap
23.	Juluki	:	A kind of fish-trap
24.	Japa	:	A kind of basket used for keeping cloth
25.	Jatar	:	A kind of weaving instrument
26.	Kula	:	Tray
27.	Khorahi	:	Small basket
28.	Karia	:	A kind of instrument used for milking
29.	Khel	:	A division of people made by the Ahom Kings for Specific profession
30.	Kahar	:	An artisan in bell – metal industry
31.	Khuka	:	A kind of fish-trap
32.	Khaloi	:	A small basket used for keeping fish
33.	Lati	:	A kind of weaving instrument
34.	Latai	:	A kind of weaving instrument
35.	Misc	:	Miscellaneous
36.	Murha	:	Stool
37.	Muhura	:	A kind of weaving instrument
38.	Mukha	:	A mask
39.	Namghar	:	A prayer hall
40.	Pachi	:	A basket
41.	Polo	:	A kind of fish-trap
42.	Palang	:	Bed
43.	Pawry	:	A kind of fish-trap
44.	Pera	:	Box
45.	Ranch	:	A kind of weaving instrument
46.	Salpira	:	Platform used for sitting

47.	Satra	:	A vaishnavite religious institution
48.	Tuna	:	A basket used for keeping fish
49.	Toka	:	A kind of musical instrument
50.	Takou	:	A kind of palm
51.	Thoura	:	A kinds of fish-trap
52.	Ugha	:	A kind of weaving instrument
53.	Visnu	:	One of the three Gods

Abbreviations

1.	AKVIB	: Assam Khadi and Village Industries Board
2.	AGMC	: Assam Government Marketing Corporation.
3.	ARTFED	: Assam Apex Weavers and Artisans Co-operative Federation.
4.	ASIDC	: Assam Small Industries Development Corporation
5.	BCDI	: Bamboo and Cane Development Institute
6.	BSI	: Bamboo Society of India
7.	BAIF	: Bharatiya Industries Foundation
8.	CTBT	: Cane and Bamboo Technology Centre.
9.	DICC	: District Industries Centre and Commerce.
10.	DC (H)	: Development Commissioner (Handicrafts)
11.	HHEC	: Handicrafts and Handlooms Export Corporation
12.	HEPC	: Handicrafts Export Promotion Council

13. INBAR : International Network for Bamboo and Rattan.
14. IIT : Indian Institute of Technology.
15. IIFT : Indian Institute of Foreign Trade.
16. KVIC : Khadi and Village Industries Commission
17. NEHHDC : North Eastern Handicrafts and Handloom Development Corporation.
18. NEDIFi : North Eastern Development Finance Corporation.
19. NER : North Eastern Region.
20. NGO : Non Governmental Organization.
21. NID : National Institute of Design
22. RFRI : Rain Forest Research Institute
23. TERI : Tata Energy Research Institute
24. UNDP : United Nations Development Programme.
25. UNIDO : United Nations Industrial Development Organization.

Photograph

A rural artisan carrying his products to the market

Bibliography

Books

1. Abraham, T.M., *Handicrafts in India*, Graphics Columbia, New Delhi, 1964.

2. Agarwal, A.K., *North-East India, An Economic perspective*, Chugh Publication, Allahabad, 1985.

3. Ahamad, Nisar, *Problems and Management of Small Scale and Cottage Industries*, Deep and Publications, New Delhi, 1987.

4. Alam, K., *The Development Experience in Assam*, Guwahati, 1983.

5. Alemchiba, M., *The Arts and Crafts of Nagaland*, Naga Institute of Culture, Govt. of Nagaland, Kohima, 1968.

6. Bahadur, Mutna, *Cane and Bamboo Craft of Manipur*, Mutua, Mutua Museum, Imphal, 1994.

7. Baishya, Prabin, *Small and Cottage Industries, A study in Assam*, Manas Publications, Delhi, 1989.

8. Barman, R.B., *Economic Development of Assam and Governance*, North Eastern Economic Association, Guwahati, 2003.

9. Barpujari, H.K., *Assam, In the Days of the company*, NEHU Publication, Shillong, 1996

10. ———— (ed.), *The Comprehensive History of Assam*, Publication Board, Assam, Guwahati, Vol. 1, 1990, III, 1994 and Vol. V, 1993.

11. Barua, Hem, *The Red River and the Blue Hill*, Lawyer's Book stall, Guwahati, 1991.

12. Barua, B.K., *A Cultural History of Assam*, Vol. I, Lawyer's Books Stall, Guwahati, 1969.

13. Baruah, S.L., *A Comprehensive History of Assam*, Munshiram Manoharlal Publishers Pvt. Ltd., New Delhi, 1985.

14. Basha Chand, S and Bhat, K.M (Ed)., *Rattan Management Utilization*, Proceeding of the Rattan (cane) Seminar India, 29-31 January 1992, Trichur, The Kerala Forest Research Institute, Peechi, 1993.

15. Bhattacharya, Sri Nath., *Rural Industrialization n India (Its Nature and Problems)*, B.R. Publishing Corporation Delhi, 1980.

16. Bhavnani, Enakshi., *Decorative Designs and Craftsmanship of India,* D.B. Taraporevala Sons and Co. Pvt. Ltd., Mumbai, 1982.

17. Borah, Kumud Chand., *Income Distribution, sarving and Expenditure Patterns in the rural Economy of Assam*, Unpublished Ph.D. Thesis, Dept. of Economics, Diburgarh, University, Dibrugarh, 1977.

18. Borboruah, Hiteswar., *Ahomar Din*, Publication Board, Assam, Guwahati, 1997.

19. Borgohain, H., *Handloom and Handicrafts of the Adis*, Directorate of Research, Govt. of Arunachal, Pradesh, Itanagar, 1995.

20. Bose, M.L., *Social History of Assam*, concept Publishing Company, New Delhi, 1989.

21. Chandra, Bipan, *The Rise and Growth of Economic Nationalism in India*, People's Publishing House, New Delhi, 1991.

22. Chapra, P.N., *Business Economics*, Kalyani Publisher, New Delhi, 1988.

23. Chattophyay, Kamaladevi, *Handicrafts of India*, Indian Council for Cultural Relations, New Delhi, 1995.

24. Chaudhary, Radhakrishna, *Economic History of Ancient India*, Janaki Prakashan, Delhi, 1982.

25. Choudury, P.C., *The History of Civilization of the People of Assam to the twelfth Century A.D.*, Spectrum Publications, Guwahati, 1987.

26. Choudury, Satyendra Narayan, *India's North-East Industrial Resources and Opportunities*, Dibrugarh, 1996.

27. Coomaraswamy, A.K., *The Arts and Crafts of India and Ceylon*, Today and Tomorrow's Printers and Publishers, New Delhi, 1971.

28. Das, A.K., *Tribal Art and Craft*, Agam Kala Prakashan, Delhi, 1979.

29. Das, Jugal., *Asamar Loka-Kala*, Publication Board, Assam, Guwahati, 196[illegible].

30. Dasgupta, K.K., *Wood Carving of Eastern India*, Firma Klm Private Limited, Kolkota, 1990.

31. Dhamaji, J., *Indian Folk Arts and Crafts*, National Book Trast, India, New Delhi, 1981..

32. Dhar, D.N., *Artisan of the Paradise, A Study of Art and Artisan of Kashmir from Ancient to Modern Times*, Bhavana Books and Prints, New Delhi, 1999.

33. Dhar, P.K., *The Economy of Assam*, Kalyani Publishers, New Delhi, 1998.

34. ————, *Indian Economy, Its Growing Dimensions*, Kalyani Publishers, New Delhi, 1998.

35. Dhingar, Ishwar. C., *The Indian Economy, Environment and Policy*, Sultan Chand and Sons, New Delhi, 2003.

36. Dubash, P.N.P., *Art in Ancient Indian Civilization*, Deep and Deep Publications, New Delhi, 1988.

37. Dutta, B., Sarma, N.C and Das, P.C., *A Handbook of Folklore Material of North East India*, ABILAC, Guwahati, 1994.

38. Dutta, P.C and Duarah, D.K (ed.), *Handicrafts of Arunachal Pradesh*, Directorate of Research, Govt. of Arunachal Pradesh, Itanagar, 1990.

39. Dutta Ruddan and Sundharam, K.P.M., *India Economy*, S.Chand and Company Ltd., New Delhi, 1999.

40. Elwin, Verrier, *The Art of the North-East Frontier of India*, North-East Frontier Agency, Shillong, 1959.

41. Gaite, S. Edward, *A History of Assam*, Lawyer's Book stall, Guwahati, 1994.

42. Ganguli, B.N., *Indian Economic Thought, Nineteenth Century Perspective*, Tata McGraw-Hill Publishing Co. Ltd., New Delhi, 1978.

43. Ganguly, J.B.(Ed)., *Marketing in North East India*, Omsons Publications, New Delhi, 1984.

44. Ghosh, N.B., *Scientific Method and Social Research*, Sterling Publishers Private Limited, New Delhi, 1992.

45. Gogoi, Lila, *Asamar Sanskite*, Banalata, Dibrugarh, 1994.

46. Gogoi, P., *Tai-Ahom Religion and Customs*, Publication Board, Assam, Guwahati, 1976.

47. Gopakkrishna, R., *Assam- Land and People*, Omsons Publications, New Delhi, 2000.

48. Goswami, P.C., *The Economic Development of Assam*, Kalyani Publishers, New Delhi,1988.

49. Guha, Amalendu, *Medieval and Early Colonial Assam, Society, Policy, Economy,* K.P. Bagchi and Company, Kolkota, 1991.

50. Gupta, R.D., *Art of Mediaeval Assam*, Cosmo Publications, New Delhi, 1982.

51. Jain, R.K., *Guide to Industries, Policies and Procedures*, India Investment Publication, Delhi, 1988.

52. Kathuria, Sanjay, *Indian Handicraft Exports, Constraints and Prospects,* Tata MaGraw Hill Publishing Company Ltd., New Delhi, 1988.

53. Khandelwal, N.M., *Working Capital Management in Small Scale Industries*, Ashish Publishing House, New Delhi, 1985.

54. Kosambi, D.D., *The Culture and Civilization of Ancient India in Historical Outline*, Vikas Publishing House Ltd., New Delhi, 1992.

55. Kothari, C.R., *Research Methodology, Methods and Techniques*, Wishwa Prahasahan, New Delhi, 1999.

56. Kuchhal, S.C., *The Industrial Economy of India*, Chaitanya Publishing House, Allohabad, 1989.

57. Lakshmans, A.C., *Rattan of South India*, Evergreen Publishers, Bangalore, 1993.

58. Mahajan, V.S. (ed.), *Studies in Industrial Economy of India*, Vol. II, Deep and Deep Publication, New Delhi, 1987.

59. Mathur, S.P., *Economics of Small Scale Industries*, Sundeep Prakashan, Delhi, 1979.

60. Mali, D.D., *Economic Problems and Planning of Assam*, Omsons Publications, New Delhi, 1989.

61. Mali, D.D., and Deka, P. (ed.), *New Industrial Policy for Village and Small Enterprises,* Omsons Publication, New Delhi, 1995.

62. Mali, D.D. and Bandopadhyay R., *Small Industry Development in North East India (Status and Strategy).,* Omsons Publication, New Delhi, 1993.

63. Mukerjee, Radhakamal., *The Economic History of* India *(1600-1800)*, Kitab Mahal, Allahabad, 1967

64. Myrdal, Gunnar, *Asian Darma*, Vol. II, Kalyani Publishers, New Delhi, 1985.

65. Nadar, N. Thanulingom, *Small Scale Industry Interrelationship with Large Scale Industry,* Rainbow Publications, Coimbatore, 1985.

66. Nath, D., *History of the Koch Kingdom (1515-1615)*, Mittal Publication, Delhi 1989.

67. Pal, M,K., *Crafts and Craftsmen in Traditional India,* Kanak Publications, New Delhi, 1978.

68. Phookan, Nilmani, *Loka Kalpadristi*, Publication Board, Assam, Guwahati, 1987.

69. Rajguru, Sarbeswar, *Medieval Asameses Society (1228-1826)*, Nagaon, 1988.

70. Rajkumar, Sarbananda, *Itishase Soaura Chashata Bachar*, Banalata, Dibrugarh, 2000.

71. Ranjan, M.P., *Rethinking Bamboo in A D 2000*, National Institute of Design, Ahmedbad, 2000.

72. Rao, A.G and Madhavi, Koli (ed.), *Bamboo Craft Design,* Industrial Design Centre, I I T, Mumbai, 1994.

73. Rao, Ramanuja, I.V and Sastry, Cherla, B. (ed.), *Bamboo, People and the Environment*, Producting of the V th International Bamboo Workshop and the IV International Bamboo Congress, Ubub, Bali, Indonesia, 19-22 June 1995, Vol. I, Propagation and Management, Vol. 4, Socio-Economic and Culture, International Network for Bamboo and Rattan, New Delhi, 1996.

74. Raychaudhuri, Tapan and Habib, Irfan (ed.), *The Cambridge Economic History of India*, Vol. I, Combridge University Press, New Delhi, 1984.

75. Saikia, Debajit, *The Problems and Prospects of Rabi Crops in the Flood- Prone Areas of Assam: A Case Study in Majuli Sub-Division*, Unpublished Ph.D.

Thesis, Department of Economics, Dibrugarh University, Dibrugarh, 2004.

76. Saikia, Rajen, *Socio and Economic History of Assam (1853-1921)*, Manohor, New Delhi, 2000.

77. Saikia, Sunil Kumar, *Small Scale Industries in Assam*, Indian Institute of Entrepreneurship, Guwahati, 2001.

78. Sanjeet (ed.), *Handicrafts India Year Book*, Handicrafts India, New Delhi, 1988.

79. Saraf, D.N., *Craft Development (1941-1991)*, Sampark, New Delhi, 1991.

80. Sarma, Satyendranath, *A Socio-Economic and Cultural History of Assam*, Guwagati, 1989.

81. ————., *The New-Vaisnavite Movement and the State Institution of Assam*, Guwahati University, Guwahati, 1966.

82. Sarma, Prabin Kumar, *Role of the Forest Resources on the Economy of Assam*, Unpublished Ph.D. Thesis, Dibrugarh University, Dibrugarh, 1986.

84. Shirali, Aditi, Textile *and Bamboo Crafts of North Eastern Region*, National Institute of Design, Ahmedabad, 1983.

85. Singh, Jai Prakash and Sengupta, Gautam (ed.), *Archaelogy of North-Eastern India*, Vikas Publishing House Pvt. Ltd., New Delhi, 1991.

86. Sing, V.B. (ed.), *Economic History of India (1857-1956)*, Allied Publishers Limited, New Delhi, 1975.

87. Singhal, R.M and Gangopadhya, P.B., *Bamboo in India and Dutta Basse*, Indian Council of Foresty Research and Eucation, Dehra Dun, 1999.

88. Swarup, Shanti, *5000 Years of Arts and Crafts in India and Pakistan*, D.B. Taraporevala Son and Co. Private Ltd., Mumbai, 1969.

89. Tarun, T.N.S., *Small Scale Industries and India's Economic Development*. Deep and Deep Publications, New Delhi, 1986.

90. Thakur, P. (ed.), *India's North-East*, Prakash Publishing House, Tinsukia, 1982.

91. Upabhya, M.N., *Economic of Handicrafts Industry*, S. Chanda and Co.(Pvt.) Ltd., New Delhi, 1973.

92. Watts, George and Brown, Percy., *Arts and Crafts of India, A Descriptive Study,* Cosmo Publications, New Delhi, 1979.

93. Wong, K.N. and Manokaran, N (ed.), *Proceeding of the Rattan Seminar*, Kulala Lumpru, Malysia, 2-4 October 1984, Forest Research Institute, Kepong, Malaysia, 1985.

Journals

1. Borah, K.C and Goswami, H., "Infrastructural Development of Assam", *Assam Economic Journal*, Vol, Xiv, Department of Economics, Dibrugarh University, Dibrugarh, 2001.

2. Farooqi, Sibghatullah "Small Scale Industries: Facing Acute Crisis," *Kurukshetra*, Vol. 51, No. I, New Delhi, 2002

3. Goswami, H and Gogoi, J.K., "Interstate Disparities in Economic Development of India with special Reference to North Eastern States," *Assam Economic Journal*, Dibrugarh University, Dibrugarh, 2001.

4. Jethra, B.D., "Export Orientation for Small and Medium Enterprise," *Yojana,* Vol. 44, No. 9, New Delhi, 2000.

5. Kharpuri, R.P., "Entrepreneurship: The Gateway to progress and Self-Reliance," *Journal of the North Eastern Council*, Vol. 20, No. 3, Shillong, 2000.

6. Khanka, S.S., "Development of Small Scale Industries in Assam," *Journal of The North Eastern Council*, Vol. 19, No. I, Shillong, 1999

7. Liebl, Maureen and Roy, Tirthankar, "Handmade in India: Preliminary Analysis of Crafts Producers and Crafts Production," *Economic and Political Weekly* , Vol. XXXVIII, Mumbai, 2003.

8. Lopoyetum, Samwel Kakuko, "Cooperative Entrepreneurship: A Perspective," *Kurukshetra*, Vol. 52, No. 1, New Delhi, 2003.

9. Mali, D.D., "A Case for entrepreneurship Education," *Journal of the North Eastern Council*, Vol. 21, No. I, Shillong, 2001.

10. Rohini, S., "Informal Sector-An Introduction," Laghu Udyog Samachar, *A Journal on Small Scale Industries*, Vol. XXIX, No. 3 to 5, New Delhi, 2004.

11. Rajyalakshim, N., "Productivity Awareness Among SSI Units: A Case Study," *The Indian Journal of Commerce*, Vol. 57, No. 2, New Delhi, 2004.

12. Sahoo, Sukanta Kumar, "Small Scale Manufacturing Industries in India," *Indian Economic Journal*, Vol. 51, No. I, Kolkota, 2003-04.

13. Vaidya, Bankimchandra, "Entrepreneurship Development: Transforming Rural Scenario," *Kurukshetra*, Vol. 52, No. 2, New Delhi, 2003.

Reports and Other Publications

1. *Assam State Gazetteer, Sivasagar District*, Govt. of Assam, Shillong, 1967.

2. *Assam State Gazetteer, Lakhimpur District*, Govt. of Assam, Guwahati, 1976.

3. *Assam State Gazetteer, Darrang District*, Govt. of Assam, Guwahati, 1978.

4. *Assam State Gazetteer*, Vol. I, Govt. of Assam, Guwahati, 1999.

5. *Assam, Beyond, 2000*, Asom Prakalpa, Guwahati, 2000.

6. *Assam 2000, A Hand Book*, Directorate of Information and Public Relation, Govt. of Assam, Guwahati, 2000.

7. *Assam Handicraft Survey*, Small Industry Extension Training Institute, North East Regional Branh, Guwahati, 1982.

8. *Assam, Handicrafts at a Glance*, North Eastern Region, Office of the Development Commissioner (Handicrafts), Ministry of Textile, Govt. of India, Guwahati, 2000.

9. *Assam's Sublime Handicrafts*, Assam Government Marketing Co-operations Ltd., Guwahati, 2003.

10. Banki, R.L., *Domestication and Improvement of Bamboo*, INBAR Working Paper No. 10, International Network for Bamboo and Rattan, New Delhi, 1997.

11. *Basic Statistic of North Eastern Region* 2000, North Eastern Council, Ministry of Home Affairs, Govt. of India, Shillong, 2000.

12. Belcher, Nrian. M., *The Bamboo and Rattan Sectors in Asia: An Analysis of Production-to-Consumption Systems*, Working Paper No. 22, International Network for Bamboo and Rattan, New Delhi, 1999.

13. Borah, K.C., Key Note Address in the UGC Sponsored National Level Seminar on *Present Status of Handicrafts in the North- Eastern Region* Held at Gargaon College, Simaluguri, 3rd and 4th February, 2006.

14. *Culture Background of Assam's Handicrafts*, Directorate of Industries, Govt. of Assam, Guwahati, 1987.

15. *Development of Bamboo and Cane Sector in India*, Ministry of Environment and Forest, Govt. of India, New Delhi, 1999.

16. *Directory of Assam Handicrafts*, Directorate of Industries, Govt. of Assam, Guwahati, 1978.

17. *Draft Annual Plan 2006-07,* Vol. II, General Areas Plan, Planning and Development Department, Govt. of Assam, Dispur.

18. *Economic Survey, Assam*, 2001-2002 and 2004-2005, Directorate of Economic and Statistic, Govt. of Assam, Guwahati.

19. *Encyclopedia Britannica*, Vol. II, INC, William Bention, Publisher, Chicago, 1966.

20. *Foreign Trade and Balance of Payments*, Centre for Monitoring Indian Economy Pvt. Ltd., Mumbai, 2003.

21. Haldar, P.K., Facets of Marketing Development of Handicrafts in the State of Tipura, First State Level

Marketing Workshop on Handicrafts of Tipura, 18th August 1998, Agartala, Office of the Development Commissioner (Handicrafts), Ministry of Textiles, Govt. of India, North Eastern Region, Guwahati, 1998.

22. *Handicrafts of Assam - A Golden Traditions*, Directorate of Industries, Govt. of Assam, Guwahati, 1987.

23. Haridasan, K., "Bamboo Based Socio-Economic Revolution in Rural Southeastern China - Relevance to North East India", *Arunachal Forest News (A Biannual Bulletin)*, State Forest Research Institute, Vol. 18, No. 1 and 2, Itanagar, 2000.

24. Hunter, W.W., *A Statistical Account of Assam*, Vol. II, B.R, Publishing Corporation, Delhi, 1975.

25. Krishnankutty, C.N., *Socio-Economic and Ecological Aspects of Developing Bamboo Resources in Homesteads of Kerala*, Part II, Economic and Management Aspects, Kerala Forest Research Institute, Peechi, 1998.

26. Mathew, P.M., *The Bamboo Economy of Kerala, India: An Analysis of the Production-to-Consumption Systems*, INBAR Working Paper No. 12, International Network for Bamboo and Rattan, New Delhi, 1998.

27. Nagi, Kanwarjit, *The Status of Bamboo Crafts in Karjat, India, and Strategies for Development*, INBAR Working Paper No. 19, International Network for Bamboo and Rattan, New Delhi, 1998.

28. *North Eastern Region, Handicrafts at a Glance, 2002*, North, Eastern Region, Office of the Development

Commissioner (Handicrafts), Ministry of Textile, Govt. of India, Guwahati, 2002

29. Prasad, Krishra Govind, Bamboo Sector Development in the North East: Challenges and Opportunities, National Workshop on *Policy and Legal Issues in Cultivation and Utilization of Bamboo, Rattan and Forest Trees in Private and Community Lands*, 7-9 August 2001, Kerala, Forest Research Institute, Peechi, 2001.

30. *Profiles on Bamboo Based Products*, Vol. I, North Eastern Council, Ministry of Home Affairs, Govt. of India, Shillong, 1996.

31. *Report of Advisory Committee on Industry*, Vol. I and II, Assam, Guwahati, 1996.

32. *Socio-Economic Issues and Constraints in the Bamboo and Rattan Sector: INBAR'S Assessment*, International Network for Bamboo and Rattan, New Delhi, Working, Paper No. 23.

33. *Statistical Hand Book, Assam*, 2001, Directorate of Economics and Statistics, Govt. of Assam, Guwahati.

34. *Study of Cane and Bamboo Reserved in North East India*, Technical Report North East Handloom and Handicrafts Development Corporation Shillong, 2001.

35. *The New Book of Knowledge*, Vol. 4, Grolier Incorporated, Connecticut, USA, 1994.

Index